Penny for Your Thoughts: Lessons Learned at a Suicide Hotline

P.M. Singer

Day One 5
Prelude in Retail 6
Getting Started 8
The Basics 12
Mental Health 101 and Advanced Suicide Studies....................................15
Frequent Flyers and Fappers..18
Innocent Fun 21
Diversion – Sullivan 23
Penny for Your Thoughts 25
Malcolm..26
Diversion – Mike 28
Abuse 30
Food Thief 33
Brief (Non) Diversion and Becoming Queen 35
Under the Gun...37
Diversion – Grad School 39
Lucky Penny 41
The Saga of Sam and Vena...47
Diversion – Grant 49
Diversion – Grant 2.0 52
Penny v. Jenna 56
A Natural Risk of the Business...60
Lacey...63
What She Did..65
A Weird Phenomenon...67
Self-Care 69
Epilogue..71

"I shall try to tell the truth, but the result will be fiction." – Katherine Anne Porter

Day One

All my training had led up to this: My first day on the crisis line. Now that I've removed my training wheels, so to speak, I'm offered the chance to change desks further away from the supervisor. I don't take it. I like my cozy, secluded little corner-cube. It's away from the gossip of the Puerto Rican Ladies and thus quieter. It allows me the privacy to read during downtime. I wouldn't trade this cube for any other.

My first call of the day, a blocked number:

"Crisis Hotline, can I – "

A clinched male voice. "I'm gonna jump!"

Though my heart is pounding, I respond as I've been trained: Try to remove the threat first. "OK, let's talk. While we're talking could you step away from the ledge so we can concentrate on what we're saying?"

The man makes a noise that isn't any particular word. "What are you talking about? I'm gonna fucking jump!"

The phone hangs up. I have no number to call back.

I check with Sam to see if I should have done anything differently. She shrugs. "Sounds like you did fine. Sometimes you just can't help what's on the other end."

I try to take her words in, but all day I can't shake the feeling that I somehow got my career as a crisis counselor off to an inauspicious start.

Today we have one of our mandatory training sessions, which means I have to stay at work several extra hours. They happen once a month or so, usually alternating between an agency in the community or a review of skills. This month it's a community agency that helps kids who are victims of abuse. Hey, just how I wanted to spend the end of this already long day, listening to graphic tales of child abuse. Still, it's important information about an agency I, of course, had no idea about until then. I figure everything will be fine once I get home. I climb into my rusty red car and pull out of the lot.

I don't get 100 yards before I see a fluttering bird in front of my windshield, then an explosion of feathers in the rearview mirror. I scream and do my best not to cry the whole way home.

This all may sound terrible – and you'd be right. But at least I got my worst day out of the way when I started off. Right?

Prelude in Retail

OK, let's rewind a bit. How did I get to this point? Well, to get to where I am now, we need to look back a little ways. Come with me back just a short nine months beforehand when I was graduating with my Bachelor's in psychology.

Like many other young people newly released into the wild from the safe captivity of college, I entered this strange, exciting, and frightening place called the Real World both fresh-faced and with a sense of entitlement. After all, all one needed to do was point to the fact that one had a college degree and one's salary would automatically be doubled; providing me with a diploma – magna cum laude no less – was the equivalent of passing an inspection with flying colors and the recommendation of all qualified experts in the field. While of course I wouldn't be able to stake out absolutely any job I wanted, the world was still, essentially, my oyster.

Clearly the rude awakening that inevitably followed was a bit unsettling.

Unfortunately, the truth is that with a Bachelor's in psychology – magna cum laude or not – one doesn't have a very broad pick of what sort of jobs for which one is considered truly qualified. Any of the "good ones" (a.k.a. more intellectual than labor-intensive, better paying) required a bare minimum of a Master's, and at $40,000 a year, I could not afford to go to the only institution that had accepted my graduate application. Grudgingly coming to terms that my last year of undergrad was spent in a self-induced state of insomnia for naught, I deferred my enrollment for six months. In the meantime, I needed to work.

I frittered away at a couple of retail jobs, the sort of entry-level bullshit that everyone has to deal when they first enter the working world. I may have been cheery on the sales floor or behind the register, but inside I was stewing in desperation. I was ready to get out and work someplace worthy of my credentials.

Since I first started working at the age of seventeen, I have absolutely hated the application process with a burning passion. I'm not sure if it's laziness on my part or perhaps some indignant feeling that people should just know that I can work or maybe even just the panic of trying to summarize myself in such a ridiculously succinct form as a résumé – I get very uncomfortable about the whole process. Needless to say online employment-search engines spoke volumes of opportunity to me: I could get my foot in the door while in my pajamas, giving me sufficient time to prepare for an in-person interview.

I fired off a few applications that I didn't care too much whether or not I actually got. One in particular, however, stood out to me. The listing was for a telecounselor at a crisis call center, where workers would, essentially, be phone operators providing information, referral, supportive counseling, and suicide prevention. Not only was this the first listing that I felt would both put my education to use and avoid difficult physical labor, but it also was the first to feel like it could be personally satisfying for me. Having struggled with my own bouts of despair, sometimes to the point of self-harm or suicidal ideations, I thought this would be truly meaningful, something I could really wrap my brain around. I took extra care with this application before shooting it off into cyber-space.

By this time summer was dwindling into the rusted hues of autumn, corroding just like my hopes of ever escaping Retail Limbo. I started to fret in an admittedly melodramatic manner that my life was doomed to be spent in a series of dead-end, unfulfilling jobs where I'd be pushing member's only specials and in-store promotions as if my very salvation depended on it.

Then a few days before Black Friday I got a call on my break requesting, then and there, for a phone interview for the call center. Luckily the break room was empty for a change, and I spent the entirety of my lunch detailing exactly why I should get that job, sometimes exaggerating my qualifications (never outright lying though) because dammit, I had some office-appropriate attire hanging in my closet and I needed a reason to wear it. I then had an in-person interview in December and in the middle of January I started my position.

As one might hope is the case for such a service, they didn't just throw us in blind, so to speak. We got a lot of training, months worth of it to slowly integrate us in, starting with the easier lines, ones that were just offering very basic referrals as to where one can find specific types of assistance, and eventually working up to the counseling and suicide prevention hotlines. We'd get programmed in to receive certain types of calls, the name of the line would come on our phone screen, and we'd answer accordingly. And it was around when I finally started taking calls that I started to realize not only how quirky the job itself was, but also just the sort of people that end up working for such an agency. Myself included, I suppose.

Getting Started

Truth be told, I never thought I'd work for a suicide hotline. Actually, when I was an undergraduate earning that precious magna cum laude, I thought I'd be a sex therapist. I took specialized courses, worked with a professor to revamp her classes on human sexuality, and applied to grad programs that focused on sex therapy. Never mind that none of those programs accepted me and I couldn't afford to go to the one program that did, even with loans – I was going to be a sex therapist someday. But I figured working at a hotline like this would give me valuable experience actually working with people, as I had yet to do that in any professional capacity.

My in-person interview was with Kathi, whose title I never quite remembered. I just thought of her as the head honcho, since that's what she was. Kathi was a frail, bird-like woman who looked like a stiff breeze might make her vanish in a crumbling puff of bone-dust. She kept her managerial distance, but she could have bouts of friendliness. A few months after I started she loaned me a book by Joan Didion that I've since recommended to others. It takes a certain trust to loan someone one of your own books, and I was flattered by it.

I made sure to drive to the building the day before my interview to be certain I knew how to get there. The day of the interview, I was told I needed to call a number to get let in. The building was locked at all times, and no one was let in unless they were previously approved of. "It sounds extreme," Kathi apologized, "but we've had a need for it over the years." She did not elaborate.

During the interview, Kathi asked the usual round of questions you get at any interview. I always imagine the people who do these interviews must know they're bullshit questions and are just trying to suss out the real idiots, but I could be wrong. Anyway, she fires off the standards and after I get through them she asks something which makes sense to me now, but at the time caught me off guard.

"Now, we're a hotline that works with the public," she begins in her reedy voice, "and a lot of our callers have mental illness. We hear every kind of terrible thing you can think of, from racist terms to admissions of child abuse. How do you think you'd handle that?"

As I said, I've had my bouts of depression as well, so technically that makes me mentally ill too. So nowadays I'd challenge Kathi: Being mentally ill doesn't make a person a racist or a child abuser or any of that. Being an asshole does. But in those days it wouldn't have occurred to me to make that distinction.

My mouth was probably dry. I don't remember, but that happens when I get nervous. When I got hired I'd always keep a water bottle at my desk. People teased me for it, but I was the one who sat there comfortably, keeping myself hydrated while they made fifty trips to the water cooler.

"Well… I mean, we're supposed to work with everyone, so whatever I felt about what they were saying, I'd have to get through it. I'd have to treat them with respect, even if I personally don't respect their opinions." I then add, "And are employees here mandated reporters of child abuse?"

"Yes, we are," Kathi says, making a note on her memo pad. "Meeke will go over that in training."

Who? What was that name? Did she say "meek?" My confusion is not evident, and she goes on to her next question.

"When you get stressed out, what do you like to do?"

I'm disarmed by this question, and it takes me a beat before I can answer. "Um. Well, I like to write. And sometimes I blast music in my car."

She sees my uncertainty and smiles. "That might seem like an odd question, but we hear a lot of stressful things, and people can get burnt out. We need to make sure we take care of ourselves so that we can help others better."

I nod. Makes sense.

"Meeke does our training," Kathi goes on, "She's wonderful. She's worked at a few different hotlines before coming to work for us, and she works part-time for another hotline as well. Meeke's training lasts a few weeks. If you're hired, you'll be in with some other new people."

She'd said the name several times now. Yes, she was saying a name that sounded like "meek." That couldn't be an American name. I had visions of an elegant woman in a sari, or perhaps an immigrant from the Far East with an accent. So when I got hired and met a woman just as pale, plump, and American as me, I was surprised. Meeke was no stranger to people getting confused by her name. Her mother was a hippie, she explained, and named her that because the meek shall inherit the earth. "Yeah," she'd add, "that kind of hippie."

Her name may have been based on a timid word, but Meeke was anything but. Meeke loved to know everything that was going on at the hotline, from what you were eating for lunch to what book I was reading during my breaks. In other people it probably would have come off as nosiness, but it just seemed smart to me: By getting into everything, she could keep her finger on the pulse of the hotline's mood. By keeping her ear out for gossip, she could learn about problems she didn't know the hotline was having. She was quite successful at bridging that gap between manager and minion.

My first lesson working at a crisis hotline: It actually doesn't pay very well, and it's pretty damn easy to get the job.

I would later learn that other hotlines were different – some didn't pay anything at all, based solely on volunteers – but when I got hired, I made the same as a cashier at the local hardware store. It always struck me that if you want employees that can talk someone down from the ledge, you should probably pay them well. Nevertheless, I couldn't complain – it was still more money than I'd been making at the various retail gigs I'd left behind.

As for how easy it was to get a job – well, I should have been grateful for that too. After all, my experience was all academic at that point, and despite the airs I put on, that meant exactly jack squat in the Real World. Sure, I could read piles of research articles in just a few hours, summarize them, and rate how helpful I thought they'd be for a class, but I couldn't tell you how to help someone experiencing active hallucinations, or where the closest food cupboard was, or even how to stop a nosebleed, let alone a cut wrist. If you asked me where to find emergency shelter for you and your family, I would have shrugged and suggested you call 911 (at least in this city, that's wrong).

By the way, that Bachelor's I put so much stock in? That wasn't even a requirement for the job. It was nice to have, but not necessary. They put a lot more stock in that vague qualifier "experience," and there were plenty of people there with not-the-best education who had loads of experience. What sort of experience? Some people worked in homeless shelters, food banks, with troubled teens, in a youth shelter, with kids who had behavioral problems, with developmentally delayed adults – in short, all things I had never done. While sticking my nose up at those who "only" had a GED, I should have been thanking my lucky stars they took me with "only" a Bachelor's.

I'll admit, there were a few people who I never quite figured out. Marisol was a shift supervisor, the one in charge of most of my direct training (Meeke's classes were a separate thing), and Sunny was one of us minions on the phone – and I don't think either of them had education or experience that would justify them getting hired. Still, Sunny always lived up to her name and was just as pleasant as could be, doing a great job with callers of all types. Marisol? Well, as a shift supervisor she mainly listened to other people's calls, and it was probably better for everyone that way.

The shift supervisors, and above them the supervisors, were all a different sort. There was Sam, for example, who other than Marisol, I worked with most frequently. Her name was Samantha, but you better not call her that. You better not call her "butch" either, though that's how most people would describe her: She wore all men's clothes, all of them stylish too, and her voice was deep enough to get her mistaken for a man more than once. Yes, she was a lesbian, and she was proud of it too, rainbows all over her car and even one tattooed on to her arm. She once said when she got married to Vena, her long-time girlfriend, they would have a rainbow theme.

There was also Maggie – not Margaret, but Maggie. That was her given name. Maggie is deceptively saccharine. She can switch from nurturer to enforcer on the turn of a dime. She and Sam are supervisors, and it couldn't be clearer how much they dislike each other. I don't think Maggie's homophobic – in her good moments she can be as warm as freshly-baked cookies – I think it really is personal, though neither of them ever let slip why.

Then there's Angelica, who is 900 years old if she's a day. But she's a skilled counselor, and a snappy dresser. In fact, she often wears fashions that I know came from the junior's department, because nowhere else makes clothes with that much glitter. Her make-up is unapologetically thick and sparkly. She has an affinity for fairies which culminates in her little poodle named Tinkerbell, who she occasionally brings in on Sundays. Even the dog is bedecked in sequins.

Sundays? you might ask. Well, yes. It's a crisis hotline, and people can be in crisis any time, day or night, weekends, holidays, etc. Therefore, like a hospital, we are open 24/7/365. I later learn some crisis hotlines, usually those that rely on volunteers, are only open for certain hours. I come to look down on those hotlines when I hear about them, or at best pity them. I was hired to work Sunday – Thursday, and while my schedule does change over the years, it always includes at least one weekend day. I don't get off any holidays unless I request them off well in advance, and even then it's not guaranteed. I will work Thanksgiving, Christmas, and New Years more than once.

The supervisors make it a point to encourage us taking time off, but then acting like it's a burden when you want to do so. Maggie is the queen of this, but everyone does it. They smile tersely, say how nice it is you're taking care of yourself, but oh gosh it's going to be really hard to fix the schedule because we're understaffed as it is. They talk about self-care. But boy, that schedule… You generally get the time off you requested, but not before hearing how difficult it was to cover your shifts.

Lesson two at the hotline: Crises don't take a vacation. Neither should you.

The Basics

I'm allowed to pick any cube I want in the office. I choose one secluded in the corner. It's right near the supervisor's desk, which I think will help me while I'm new.

Marisol is in charge of my daily training while Meeke will be running a sort of workshop for other new-hires and me. Marisol largely has me listening on to other people's calls and practice looking at the database we use both to log our calls and to get information on community resources. I don't know about other hotlines, but here we log every call somewhere. It might be something basic like "Caller needed number to food banks." The more complicated the call, the more complicated the notes. We do this in case the caller calls back, we can get a head's up in the notes from previous calls. It sounds kind of complex, but it's really not.

There's also an even more practical reason behind all this: On the off-chance that our records are ordered for a court hearing (this has apparently happened in the past), we can have a hopefully objective record of what transpired. The idea that this could happen drills into me the motto "If you didn't write it down, it never happened." I am perhaps a bit too anal in my note-taking. My higher-ups usually commend me for my thoroughness, but other times they complain I'm being too wordy. I prefer to err on the side of caution.

People that worry about privacy – people that include me, I'll add – might worry that their calls are being recorded, like when you call for customer support. At least when I start there, we don't record calls. We don't have the technology or the desire to do so. I don't know about other places; maybe they do, maybe they don't. Really, if you're in the position where you need to call one of these hotlines, shouldn't you be more worried about how you're doing than about what if some company might have an internal recording of your call?

Oh, another note on privacy: We have call ID, but if you block your number we can't see it. A handful of hotlines have the technology to see your number even if you do block it, but we aren't one of them. If we have your number and you're putting yourself or someone else at risk, we can try to use that number to trace your call. We don't like having to do this, but if lives are at stake, we will. It's actually pretty haphazard as to whether it works or not. I imagine – or I hope, at least – that 911 would be able to trace you a lot easier than we can. I've witnessed one trace taking upwards of an hour; thankfully the telecounselor was able to keep the caller on the line that long to keep him safe.

Anyway, you probably noticed the examples I gave above just involved someone looking for human services help. That's because although we were a crisis line, we also answered some lines that were basic informational lines – things like "where can I get food now that my food stamps ran out?" or "my power's going to be shut off, can anyone help me?" When we were new, we'd start on these lines before we graduated to the crisis line.

If you ever need to call one of these lines, it's pretty simple. Places around the country have a program called 2-1-1 and there are plenty of locally-based lines that do the same service. You tell them what you're looking for – and here's a tip: It needs to be human services related, not a business that you'd get on 411 or a person's phone number or a private office of a doctor. Basic things like "where can I get free counseling?" or "I need to find my closest AA meeting." The person on the other line – the telecounselor, as we're called – will ask you a few basic questions. Some are so they can help you out, some are just for statistics so we can tell the people who fund us who we're serving. Our big three questions were zip code, age, and how the caller heard about the line.

Oh – and you're calling to get phone numbers. Have a fucking pen and paper ready. I can't tell you how many times people have made me wait because they called me unprepared. And for Christ's sake, don't call when you're in the bathroom. That's just nasty.

During all this, I came to know my coworkers a bit better. I already mentioned the supervisors and shift supervisors, but most of us were minions, the foot soldiers actually on the phones taking the calls. There was Laura, who got hired shortly before I did. She was maybe twenty years my senior and possibly the kindest person I'd met. Laura, along with Missy, who I worked with on Sundays, became a pair who I'd come to refer to as my Work Moms. They'd fuss and dither over me, and I secretly loved it.

There was a small group in the opposite corner of the cube farm who I thought of as the Puerto Rican Ladies. Marisol would be with them, but she was a supervisor and got "The Big Girl Chair" at the head of the office. Sunny was with them, as well as a handful of others. The loudest was Zelda. No one can ignore Zelda unless she wants to be ignored. Brash, bold, and busty, she can get on your nerves at times, but you also can't help but like her. Her skills as a counselor are highly variable: Sometimes she gets in the zone and does an amazing job helping people in crisis, but just as often she's obnoxious to the callers who aren't shy complaining about her. Despite being a smaller city, we have a fair amount of Spanish-speakers, and the Puerto Rican Ladies help the rest of us out when we get these calls so we don't have to call a translation service.

There's Doris, who I swear must have babysat Moses. Unlike most of the others, she only answers the informational lines, not the crisis line. I count this as a blessing. She's sweet, but doddering, easily confused by any change. I shudder to think how she'd react on the phone to anyone truly in crisis.

I meet John, one of only about three men who work for the hotline, on Sunday. He once considered joining the priesthood. He used to work for an agency that helps kids with behavioral and psychological problems, but now by day he sells sound systems. He works here part-time. We accidentally get off on the wrong foot when I comment how fake, and therefore silly, wrestling is.

"How can you say that?" he demands. "I'm not saying it isn't scripted, but so's everything else you see on TV. The sheer athleticism – the physicality to do the moves, the stunts, I just…" He trails off in frustration, shaking his head.

Angelica, who is supervising that day, glances at me meaningfully and smiles. Her lipstick is a shimmery pink.

Then there is Jenna.

Jenna was hired only a month before me, but she had the jaded sense of ennui of someone who had worked there for years. I'll come right out and say it: I don't like Jenna. She's crass and crude, an overly familiar sort of joking that rubs me entirely the wrong way. At first, I think I'll get used to it – she e-mails me some nasty comment about a fellow new-hire, Ellie, and I admit, I laugh. But I never get used to it. She just seems mean-spirited and spiteful.

Neither she nor her husband ever cooked dinner, going out to eat literally every night. This might be normal in big cities like New York, but in our little rust belt city it was an odd quirk, especially for someone who constantly claimed to be on a diet. She is always doing some home improvement project on her home or planning a vacation, and I do not exaggerate when I say "always." In the entire time I work with her, I don't remember any time she wasn't doing one or the other, or both.

Because of all this, I took this to mean she had been born with a silver spoon in her mouth. I later learn it's quite the opposite: She had a pretty lousy childhood and was lucky to even get her Associate's degree. It does explain, I think, why she can be so blunt – not just to coworkers, but to callers. If she can make it through the other side of a shitty upbringing, why can't they?

The classes that Meeke gives I take with Ellie, Jenna, Laura, and another new hire named Alex, who I swear has some sort of mental disorder himself, maybe Asperger's or something, because of his oddness. I find the classes fascinating because we finally delve into the nitty-gritty of what working at a crisis hotline actually entails – at least, the mental health aspect, the part that interested me in the first place. Finally I was going to learn what made this place tick.

Mental Health 101 and Advanced Suicide Studies

Part of our training with Meeke involved some basic overviews of mental disorders. Our role as telecounselor was never to diagnose anyone. The purpose of this part of training was strictly to give us a working understanding of various disorders since callers would often disclose diagnoses to us.

Jenna and Alex were at a disadvantage here. Ellie was a nurse, Laura had her Master's, and even in my Bachelor's program we had an overview of "abnormal psychology." But I'm pretty sure I had a leg up on all of them in another way: I doubt any of them had ever seen a shrink because they nearly killed themselves.

I had just turned fifteen. Even though I had just entered the high school, I couldn't say anything else had changed in particular. Except it had. It was hard to put into words. I didn't have emotions so much as an all-enveloping numbness. When I managed to break through that empty feeling, I felt teary and overwhelmed. I was afraid of much. Sleep wasn't restful, but at least it offered me the solace of avoiding my feelings, or rather my lack of them.

I don't remember how I thought of it, but I decided to cut myself. Before I did it, I thought it through to make sure I'd do it in a place that would never be seen, not even in the changing room for gym class. I finally decided on my hip, reasoning that it would always be covered with my underpants (I wasn't the sort who was taking her panties off at that age). I didn't cut deeply or anything – in fact, I barely broke the surface of the skin – but it was enough. It hurt, and hurting was feeling something and therefore was better than that muffled cloud of nothingness. I relied on it every day, dragging the pin through the open wound for every thing I had done wrong that day. I'd always give myself one extra for the sheer sin of living.

I went months through that fog, the thick, gummy muck of depression. And finally I had enough. I had been limping along for so long I didn't see that life was ever going to get any better. If these were the best years of my life, what fresh new hell lay before me in the coming years?

I wrote notes to say goodbye. I got a rope. I decided on a day. But when the time came, I found I was too afraid to follow through with my plans.

Cutting myself became less frequent, but a little deeper. I had found a Swiss Army Knife in the house, and I hid it in my room. I still only cut superficially, but it hurt more. Maybe it was the sting of being forced to live a life that I felt I wasn't supposed to be living.

My parents were in the dark about all this. They knew I was withdrawn, but they attributed it to the moody growing pains of adolescence. But I finally gave in and told a friend about all this; she told a school counselor, and she told my parents. They both cried when talking to me, and I cried too. I had spent so long worried about what would happen if I was found out that now I was terrified I'd be locked away in a mental ward.

My fears were unfounded, but I was taken to a counselor. Her office was in blah pastel tones. She asked me if I heard voices. I laughed nervously when I told her, truthfully, that I didn't. I was worried she wouldn't believe me. She referred me to a psychiatrist who had me look at ink-blots. I saw her once a week for several months.

So when Meeke pulls out her charts and statistics on Major Depressive Disorder, I allow my mind to wander a bit. I don't need to know the numbers, I've been among them.

We cover other mental disorders, of course. Bipolar Disorder. Schizophrenia. Borderline Personality Disorder. These will become part of our vernacular.

We move on to the topic of suicide itself. Some statistics first:

As of writing this, suicide is the tenth leading cause of death in the US. Although anyone can and does complete suicide, there are some risk factors. People with mental illness are at higher risk for suicide, as are LGBT people, especially LGBT youth. There is some increased risk among the elderly, who often visit their doctors before completing suicide. Women are more likely to attempt, but men are more likely to complete suicide since they tend to use deadlier means.

You'll have noticed my use of the term "completed suicide." That's considered the appropriate thing to say rather than "committed suicide." Suicidologists (yes, there is such a thing) say using the term "committing suicide" only further marginalizes the issue by talking about it like it's a crime. "Died by suicide" is also acceptable.

There are "suicidal gestures," which are indications that a person plans on ending his life. He might give away beloved possessions, talking about how he doesn't need them anymore. He might cut off ties with friends and loved ones. He might write notes saying his goodbyes.

We also discuss "suicide attempts," which is doing anything that a person believes will end his life. It can be definitely deadly acts, like cutting his wrists, but it can also be something like taking one too many Tylenol, which probably won't do any harm. If the person believes it will end his life, it's considered a suicide attempt. The term suicide attempt is used to differentiate from self-harm, which is simply injuring oneself on purpose and might, unintentionally, result in suicide.

There are different levels of "being suicidal," as it turns out. One isn't more valid than the other, but combinations of them can be lethal. The most common is suicidal ideation, which is any of the thoughts people have of suicide from anything as vague as "Maybe I'd be better off dead" to the more concrete "Next Tuesday I'm going to kill myself." The three keys to risk are plan (how definite is it?), means (can the person access something that can end his life?), and intent (does the person intend to act on these thoughts of suicide?).

Maybe other hotlines have this, but our hotline has some slang around suicide.

The most common one you hear is a "light suicide" versus a "heavy suicide." Light suicides are pretty common: They're the people who are somewhat suicidal, but not really at risk. Heavy suicides are either actively involved in harming themselves right now, or they are at serious risk to do so soon.

Some people are chronically suicidal at varying degrees of severity. Some people think about suicide every day but won't ever attempt it, thinking of suicide more as an escapist fantasy than any real option. Some people attempt multiple times, each time with the real intent to die. Ellie raises her hand.

"There are also people who attempt and they expect they'll be saved at the last minute," she adds.

"Sure," Meeke concedes. "There are people who do that."

Ellie has barely allowed Meeke the response. "When I worked at the hospital, we had a guy who was like that. He did all these things to himself and then he'd call 911 on himself." I expect that to be it, but she goes on, "Yeah, but then finally he did it. He drank a bunch of bleach and there was nothing we could do. He was begging us, 'I don't really want to die!' but it was too late. It was awful. He was bleeding out of his eyeballs."

I suddenly decide I don't like Ellie. If I have a caller who has drunk bleach, the last thing I need is that visual, let alone the knowledge that no matter what I do it will be in vain.

During one of the breaks, I gather my courage and approach Meeke away from the other attendees. I ask her if someone has the plans, means, and intent to act on her suicidal ideation, but then suddenly changes her mind, would that be considered a gesture or an attempt. She doesn't have a definitive answer, saying she could argue for either one. She shrugs and says it would still be someone who certainly needed help. I merely nod and agree.

Frequent Flyers and Fappers

I didn't know it when I began, but Meeke, who has worked at various hotlines over the years, explains: "Every crisis hotline gets repeaters," she says, "It's like a hospital like that. Some places call them frequent flyers." Ellie nods sagaciously. I don't really dislike Ellie, but she gets on my nerves easily, mainly because she wears far too much perfume. She constantly reeks of musk and pepper. Shortly after our hiring, a "friendly reminder" e-mail is sent out to remind people not to wear too much perfume/cologne. It has no effect.

Repeaters, Meeke goes on, can become such for various reasons. Sometimes they have poor connections to mental health services, and rely on us for some semblance of counseling. In that case we're to provide support, but encourage linkage to counseling or case management, etc. Generally, however, we're a tool they use in between meetings with their various professionals.

Sometimes they have no friends and think of the hotline workers as friends. Meeke reminds us we are under no circumstances to become pally with repeaters. "We are professionals, and we have a professional relationship with them. We might become fond of certain repeaters, but we aren't really their friends." It seems like this should go without saying, but apparently this became a problem in the past: Apparently a former employee once broke protocol entirely and located a repeater's home, an offense for which she would have been fired had she not quit. This former employee became friends with this repeater because she felt sorry for the woman not having any friends.

Anyone is free to call the hotline as often as they want – up to a point. Some people called so frequently that it really wasn't healthy to allow them to stay on the phone with us all the time. Some were disruptive when they called, being abusive, but just as many called just to chit-chat with us rather than calling when in some sort of crisis. Therefore some frequent flyers called frequently enough to warrant limits on their calls: Usually two calls a day, ten minutes or less per call. Some people were so abusive they only got one five minute call per day. If they called more than that, unless they were in major crisis, they would gently be redirected back to their various coping skills and the call would be ended.

As I say, some people called just to talk about mundane things. There was Millie, a developmentally delayed woman who would always open her calls with "So how are you?" before telling us about her various appointments and what she would have for lunch that day. Sometimes she'd talk about her pet goldfish. There was Max, who fancied himself something of a ladies man, who'd talk about his dating escapades. He also talked about his lunch. I have no idea why food was such a popular topic with so many of our repeaters, but it really was a trend.

I remember getting a call from Roger, a man with paranoid schizophrenia which involved delusions of persecution. He rambled on about how his television was watching him and broadcasting his thoughts to the world. He then asked my name, which I told him. He told me I was the best person at the hotline and that he would use his powers to help me become in charge of the entire hotline – he used his powers to get Bush elected, so he could promote me easily. It was not until later I learned he liked me so much because I accidentally gave him an extra call that day.

A woman named Jan had some sort of impulse control disorder. She would call us with minor frustrations, shouting vulgarities at us but always clarifying "I'm not saying them at you." Gary the Gambler spent his sparse social security paycheck on lotto tickets. Rosie has a form of OCD that makes her constantly see sexual innuendos in innocent phrases and gestures, and she calls us for reassurance that "it's just in my head, right?" Charlie used to be a sex addict, and as a result we occasionally have to ask him if he's masturbating when he's talking to us.

Charlie isn't even that odd of a case. We have several repeaters who call us for the sole purpose of masturbating. The weirdest is the one guy whose name we've never gotten because he's too busy trying to get us to say one woman's name over and over again as he pants into the phone. And before you think this is a quirk to repeat callers, we had plenty of one-time callers with dirty minds too. I can honestly say it never occurred to me that people would call a crisis hotline to get their rocks off, but Meeke pointed out during training: "We're a captive audience. We really want to help people, so we're more apt to stay on the line. And they often start innocently enough – 'I really need to talk,' or 'Can I talk about anything here?' 'It's really embarrassing.'"

One time I'm on lunch at the same time as Meeke. Somehow it comes out that I always thought I'd be a sex therapist. We get on the topic of sex callers, as we refer to them. "I'd totally work for a sex hotline," Meeke whispers. "It's gotta pay better than crisis work." I have to admit, if I'm going to have people jerking off to my voice, I'd rather know about it from the get-go.

The first time I had a sex-caller, I was so naïve. I may have been told about the possibility, but the reality had not occurred to me. I figured I would just know, that it would be obvious.

Well, it was obvious. But I was dense.

The phone rang. I answered. I whiny male voice answered, "Hey. I heard I could talk to you guys about anything?" I confirm this is true.

"I need to talk about something. It's really embarrassing."

This was literally an example we used in our training about sex callers. But I didn't hear warning bells. I heard someone in need of a listening ear.

"I went to a party this weekend. It was, like… A sort of sex party. Is that OK?"

I remember that I used to aspire to be a sex therapist, so I knew I had to be comfortable with all sorts of sexual escapades. I tell him that I think it's OK.

"Oh man, you're so cool… But more stuff happened at the party. Like…" A heaved breath. "You know… Sort of like a dildo… But with a horse tail on the end. Do you know what I mean?"

I've watched HBO's Real Sex. I know exactly what he's talking about.

"Ohh, you're so cool… Well this girl… She was using it. On me. Fucking me with it. And I really got off. Is that OK?"

"Well," I begin, not really sure what to say, but wanting to be accepting. "I mean, everyone's different. If you and your partner were willing adults, then that's OK."

"Ohhhh you're so cool," he moans before abruptly straining, "Oh God, I'm coming…"

The phone hangs up. On his end. I have just unintentionally brought a caller to climax.

Lesson: Some days you will want to take a shower at the end.

Innocent Fun

Just like I had never imagined people would call a suicide hotline with the intention to jerk it, it also never occurred to me that people would prank a suicide hotline. Again, call me naïve – I mean, I knew people would call 911 inappropriately, so why not a suicide hotline? I guess in my mind, people would have standards of decency, but time and again this has not been borne out by reality, so I was bound for a shock.

For the most part, these were just some stupid kids having a bit of innocent fun. Why they chose the suicide hotline and not, say, the local pizza place is beyond me. But we had a few calls of "Is your refrigerator running?" and similarly overplayed chestnuts. Usually you'd tell them "This is a serious line" and they'd be sufficiently shamed. If some kids kept pranking, sometimes old-timers like Missy would take advantage of the fact that we had their number on call ID. She's read the number out loud to them and ask "Should I send the police there?" That would usually get them to leave us be.

Those were the kids. There were also adults. The difference was in the execution.

This was around the time when Internet sound boards were becoming a novelty: Basically it would have sound clips from a certain celebrity, or sound effects, and you could click them for a quick prank of your friends. I know in college I did it more than once to friends – but again, friends, not a suicide hotline. I talked to Jack Nicholson multiple times. Miss Cleo, the psychic hotline lady, at least once. I think even Jim Carrey.

Those weren't really the standouts. The real assholes were the ones who used sound effects. Why? Because they included sound effects of a gun being fired.

Thankfully I knew about the existence of sound boards and I had been warned that we'd occasionally get bombarded with pranks from these cretins, so I recognized that it wasn't a real gunshot – eventually. I stayed on the phone until I heard the giggling laughter. At which point I had to announce to anyone listening, "This is a serious line; please only call back if you're in serious crisis."

If you're wondering why I didn't follow Missy's lead, the reason is twofold: One, the adults were usually savvy enough to know how to block their caller ID. So no phone number to use to scare them into submission.

Secondly, Missy's method was quite frowned upon. It was actually contrary to what we were supposed to do, which was to simply tell them this is a crisis line and to invite them to call back when they were in crisis. After all, you never know if someone is pranking the hotline simply because they're a jerk or because they are feeling out how a hotline's responders react to strange things. Today's prank-caller might be tomorrow's person in crisis.

Here's my take: If you want to feel things out at a crisis hotline, don't be an asshole scaring the shit out of them with fake gunshots or an idiot using ridiculous sound boards. That makes them hate you. Just call them and tell them why. It's seriously as simple as that. We'd even rather you call and hang up than pranking us.

Think of it this way: Every time you prank, you're taking time away from someone who actually fucking needs help. Do you feel like a big man in front of your friends now? You just stopped a hungry child's parent from getting food resources, or a person in need of counseling from getting it, or worse still, a person who might be considering suicide from getting talked out of it. Is that really how you want to spend your free time, being that guy who stops people from getting help they're reaching out for?

Yeah. I didn't think so.

Diversion – Sullivan

I met my first great love when I was barely nineteen years old. Now at twenty-two, I'm convinced I will never love again.

His name was Sullivan. We met at college through a mutual friend. He was instantly charming, literally charming the pants right off of me, no mean feat for someone who just months earlier had been uncomfortable with her boyfriend copping a feel over her shirt. When we kiss, I'm awkward and he's patient. But he partied too hard his first year and was in danger of not coming back for a second. Due to the practicalities of staying together over a long distance, we broke up. It was the first of ultimately three break-ups we had.

The second came after he did, in fact, come back for a second year of college, just minus the scholarship he had started with. We got back together immediately and were happy for a few months – or at least, I was happy. I found out he was lying to me and had been cheating on me.

The third came after I took him back.

He was contrite and admitted he didn't deserve to be taken back. But oh, how my heart had ached for him, and how lonely I felt. I had tried dating that summer, a sweet guy named Mike, but that too had fizzled back into friendship. I was just about convinced I was unlovable when Sullivan came crawling back. I helped him back on to his feet, wrapped my arms around him, and we carried on just as happily as we could. Even when I graduated, we weren't going to be over: I had applied to – and been accepted to – grad school close to his home town, so we would still be together. Forever.

Except I had no way to pay for school. Making minimum wage is no way to pay for grad school, even with loans. So again, out of necessity, we broke up.

It was sheer hopefulness on my part, but I felt the door had been left open to visits. I don't even remember why. Perhaps he'd said some vague comment like "Maybe I'll come see you," nothing with any commitment behind it, but enough to dangle a carrot of hope before my desperate eyes.

I convinced myself that he was going to visit over a weekend in April. I had talked with him about coming and for some reason, I told myself he would come. Never mind that he didn't give me a definitive "yes," never mind that he had no disposable income, and never mind that he had never been the sort to spring romantic surprises on me. But I was sure of it. He would come. And I would be ready.

I wore my favorite office outfit, a long grey skirt, a button-down blue shirt, and knee-high black boots. Beneath it I wore the most painfully lacy bra I owned and its matching panties. All day I felt extra confident on the phones, feeling delightfully taboo in my secret attire.

Of course he didn't show up. If I had been thinking logically, I would have known he wouldn't. But love makes idiots of us all, and I was no exception. I was utterly guileless in the face of my first romance, and now that it was obviously Over, I had no idea how to deal with it.

When I came home I switched my lacy underthings for a practical cotton number and a T-shirt from college. I willed myself not to cry, but eyes aren't exactly things to order around, and they stubbornly insisted on weeping. I would withdraw from the world. If I couldn't have the man I wanted, no man would have me. It would prick at my heart, slowly but steadily as a sewing machine, and it would mend the pieces of my heart back together.

I decide it's time to re-apply to grad schools I can actually afford.

Penny for Your Thoughts

A side-note: Many people at the hotline didn't use their real names on the phone. Some did this because they had unique names, like Zelda. Meeke says that when she answers the phones (only in times of dire need) she uses a fake name because too often the call would become about her weird name and distract from the caller's initial reason for reaching out. Others did it simply for reasons of privacy, like Jenna. I could get in to who had what fake name, but it really would just muddle things. Just trust me when I say about half the people I talk about weren't using their real names.

As for me, I called myself Penny. You know, "Penny for your thoughts?" Oh hush, I thought it was clever.

But using a pseudonym was no guarantee that calls wouldn't end up being about your name. Frequently I'd get asked, "Penny? What, is that short for something?" One of our repeaters, a drunk philosopher named Pauline, slurred, "Penny? What sort of name is that? What I mean is, where did it come from, like etymologically?" I'd be left to simper, "It's just Penny."

John, the would-be priest who admired wrestling, loved my new name. He said it reminded him of watching *Inspector Gadget* with his kids, Gadget's smart niece being named Penny. I kind of laughed it off, but sure enough that same day I got a call from frequent flier James, a young, delusional person who rarely made any sense on his calls.

"Crisis Hotline, may I help you?"

"You're new, who is this?" Frequent flyers either loved or hated new people. Sometimes they could get extra calls, but sometimes they preferred the staff they already knew.

"My name is Penny."

"Penny? Yo man, like *Inspector Gadget*?" He then shouted the tones to the Inspector Gadget theme song into my ear before cackling and hanging up.

I told John, who laughed. Every time we worked the same shift, he'd start humming the theme song to me as well. Eventually I started adding in the "boop-boo!" at the end.

Malcolm

Meeke and Kathi may have been in charge, but they weren't the head of the company, not by a long shot. In fact, the hotline was just one cog in an elaborate machine of human services. The biggest part of the company was a healthcare agency that worked with a couple of local hospitals, one urban and one rural, as well as some agencies that helped place people with disabilities in jobs.

This meant two things. One, we worked closely with the hospitals' psychiatric departments. Primarily we worked with their psychiatric emergency rooms, which also had mobile units that could visit clients in their homes. Once upon a time, long before I was hired, we had the same offices as one of the psych EDs, so it wasn't uncommon for people to call us trying to reach them. We'd transfer the call accordingly.

Secondly, and more importantly, we had a lot of coworkers who had disabilities. In the rural psych ED, one of the workers was hearing impaired. One of the part-time evening workers, Janice, used a wheelchair. We even had a few visually impaired workers who relied on adaptive technologies to enlarge their computer screens. Then we hired Malcolm, who was totally blind.

I didn't really like Malcolm, I'll admit it. He smelled funny and he was rude. He would eat at his desk loudly. He made a mess, a mess he couldn't see and therefore couldn't clean up.

By the way, this wasn't a problem with any of our other coworkers with visual impairments. Every other one of them was just as courteous as the average Joe. This was strictly an issue with Malcolm. He was a pig, but it was mainly just irritating, nothing you could do anything about.

Then the incident happened.

By some luck, the incident happened on a day I wasn't working for some reason. But by then it had already entered hotline legend. It was towards the end of Malcolm's shift, and he excused himself to the bathroom. He finished his shift and left. Someone else went into the bathroom, and a scream was heard by those working on their calls.

Malcolm had left a steaming turd on the toilet seat. I can't even figure out how. I've never been a hoverer, and he had to have hovered long enough to let out a sizeable poop, and by then wouldn't you feel that your aim was off? Like, wouldn't you wonder why you didn't hear even the littlest splash? Or by then was he too embarrassed and just hoped no one would go in there? My mind refuses to try to work its way around it.

A few days later, Malcolm no longer worked for us. I don't think he was fired, but merely reassigned. I hope whoever got him was warned about the reasons for his transfer.

As for that fateful shit, I don't know who took care of it, or how. I hope whoever it was didn't leave it for the janitorial staff, but I know if it was me I probably would have done just that. I don't get paid nearly enough to deal with that.

Diversion – Mike

I met Mike when we were both new hires at one of my retail jobs. It might have had something to do with the fact that I was coming off a bad break-up (Sullivan's second), but Mike struck me as a great guy. He was studying technology at a local college and had a contagious laugh. He was definitely more thoughtful than Sullivan had been, though to be fair that wasn't too hard.

We tried dating that summer, but when I went back to college four hours away, he broke up with me. We remained friends, even as I went back to Sullivan. Even as Sullivan and I had our third break-up. Even as it was obvious I was holding on to memory of Sullivan longer than was strictly healthy. Then one night Mike and I were hanging out, and I felt his arm around my shoulder, and I knew I was falling for him all over again.

He was taking summer classes and working as a tour guide to the college. I joked I would come on campus, posing as a new freshman, and insist only he give me the campus tour. We'd kiss, and he was awkward while I was patient. He was invariably done with his day the same time as me, so I'd come over from the hotline still dressed in my office attire and we'd go about our time together. We didn't do a whole lot more than hang out with our mutual friends and explore new restaurants, but still nursing the wounds of my final breakup with Sullivan, I was all right with taking things slow.

We got tickets to the touring production of *The Lion King* along with his roommate. I was a little annoyed his roommate had managed a way to tag along to what I considered our nicest date yet, but I figured we'd make it work – hadn't we always? I held his hand during "Can You Feel the Love Tonight?" and he limply held it back. After the show we went to a diner, and his roommate expressed envy at the sort of relationship Mike and I had. I beamed, and Mike blushed.

We went back to Mike's apartment, and I expected something romantic. I went in to kiss him. He sharply turned his head away, forcing me to kiss his cheek.

"I get the cheek?" I demand.

Mike stares at me dumbly.

"OK… Well… Good night, I guess." I turn on my heel sharply and slam the door behind me.

The next day Mike does me the respect of actually telling me that he thinks we worked better when we were just friends. Which I suppose I better than I ever got from Sullivan, but again, that doesn't take much work. After a period of mourning, Mike and I are able to go back to being friends effortlessly.

But I retreat further into my shell. I promise myself I'll never go out of it again. It may be dark and cold, but it's safe. Besides, grad school will be starting soon. Why bother trying to make a connection when it will be pushed aside to make room for classes? It would be best to get used to the idea of being alone, at least for now.

Abuse

I come in for the day and Camille is snoozing at her desk. I don't mean that metaphorically; she was actually sleeping at her desk. Camille worked two full-time jobs to help pay for her kids' college, working with the hotline on overnights. Generally overnights were slower, but they were staffed with fewer people, so if you worked overnights, at some point you would work with Camille.

Camille was one of those love her/hate her sort of people, both for coworkers and callers. Clearly she was a hard worker – actually, despite frequently sleeping at her desk, she always woke right up for a call, a fact that impressed her fellow overnighters. But she was also a loudmouth and a gossip. She had emigrated here from France when she was a child, and she only had the barest wisp of an accent. She was my mom's age, but looked much younger.

The other overnight worker there that morning – there's usually only two of them – is Pat, a big, black woman who loved her cigarettes. Years of smoking had deepened her voice to something like broken glass dragged over a gravel driveway. I imagine she used to be pretty when she was younger, but the smoke has prematurely aged her.

"You got to hear what happened!" Pat calls to me once I get settled in. "You know Bob?"

Bob's a frequent flyer. Most of us dread getting Bob because he's the angriest sonuvabitch we've ever met. He calls to vent his frustrations in language that offends even us, not hesitating to use slurs of every shade. If he doesn't like our comments, he'll easily turn his vitriol towards us. Because of his high propensity to become abusive to our staff, he's limited to two calls a day, ten minutes each – which he knows we will end if he starts to attack us.

"Well, Camille got him around one or so."

Camille drowses awake, hearing her name. She doesn't miss a beat though, and immediately takes over the story. "You know how he gets. Well, he's talking F-this, F-that, and you know he doesn't like Pat." I didn't, but she goes on anyway. "Well, he says 'I like you, Camille, you're not like that nigger Pat.'"

I suck my breath through my teeth. We hear a lot of nasty words, but somehow that word still makes me wince when I hear it.

"Right? So I say to him, 'How dare you, Bob? How do you know I'm not black?' He says I didn't sound black, and I ask him what 'black' sounds like. He didn't have an answer to that."

"So he calls back," Pat wheezes, "And this time I get him. And he says to me he likes 'that nice black girl Camille.'" She cackles so hard you can hear the phlegm rattle in her throat. "I asked her, 'girl, when did you change races?'"

I'm laughing too. Camille just smiles and shrugs. That's one of the things I like about Camille: She doesn't stand for abuse of anyone.

Finally my phone rings. I answer it. A hesitant female voice, young.

"Yes, ma'am. I want to know how to put your kid into foster care."

At first I think it's going to be an easy call. This is, surprisingly, not a very uncommon question, parents looking to "do something" with their unruly kids. Sometimes they're looking for a Scared Straight-sort of program. I think all this within the half a second or so that she pauses, but she keeps talking.

"My daughter was just returned to me from foster care, and it's not working out, and I think it's best if she goes back."

OK, a bit more unusual. Still, I get the usual information I need. I expect her to get irritable and demand the number, but she doesn't. In fact, she keeps talking.

"I did some bad stuff that got her taken away from me. And she's only been back a few days, and I've already done some bad stuff to her again."

A beat. I ask as casually as I can, "Can I ask what sort of bad stuff?"

I expect her to hold back, as her voice has been a bit tremulous up until now. Instead, she grows bolder. "Well, last time, when she got taken away? She was acting up and I was whupping her with my belt. But this time I didn't use my belt. I just used my hands and whupped her that way. I didn't leave any marks or anything, but I still gave her a whupping. And – " Her voice gets quavery again. "So I have mental illness OK?"

Personally, I think anyone who would whup a child with a belt definitely is some sort of crazy, so I'm not too surprised. "OK," I reply calmly.

"And I hear voices, OK? And they tell me the Devil's in my daughter. That's part of why I whup her, y'know? To beat the Devil out of her. But this time…" She trails off.

"This time it was different," I offer.

"Yeah." I hear her swallow. "I put a little bit of bleach into her milk this morning. Not a lot or anything, and as soon as she tasted it she wouldn't drink it anymore. But I made her drink some of it." She sighs. "I know that ain't right, so I want her to go back to foster care."

"Well," I begin, knowing I need to keep this woman's tenuous trust, "I think it's definitely good that you recognize that. I have the number here," I lie, looking instead at the number for mandated reporters of child abuse, "but if you'd like, I can help you out and also take your information now, and I can call them to report what's going on." I pause a moment and add, "I should let you know that I'd need to report this as abuse." Technically, I don't need to tell her this, but I don't like to mislead people.

I worry that I've pressed my luck. I worry that the woman will hang up and I'll only have a phone number to give the child abuse hotline.

Instead, "Yeah. That would be easier."

I try not to sigh in relief. I ask her name, her child's name, her address, etc – any sort of pertinent information. She gives it readily. I read and re-read over it, trying to make sure I have everything I could possibly need to report the abuse. Then, unwillingly, I let her off the phone and reassure her I'll take care of it. She thanks me.

I'm not sure about other hotlines, but as Kathi told me during my interview, those of us at this hotline are mandated reporters of child abuse. If we have any question about what to report, we're to discuss the issue with anyone above us. Sam has just sauntered in, but I simply ask her where the proper forms are because I intend to call in the report, whatever she says. When she hears why, she waves me ahead. "Yeah, some cases are vague, but that's not even a question," she says.

I call the child abuse hotline, and I'm actually able to answer every question they have. I'll have to call the reporting hotline other times in the future, and no other time do I have much information to provide them given that we're an anonymous hotline. Later in the day, Meeke pulls me aside.

"That girl you called the report on?" she says. "I got a call from CPS. They've removed her from the home."

I nod. I'm glad to hear it, and it must show.

"I read that call when I saw the report you made. You did a good job on it. You really built that rapport and made her trust you."

Lesson: Sometimes you need to build a rapport with disgusting people for a greater cause.

Lesson: I may work at a suicide hotline, but there are other ways I can help make people safe.

Food Thief

We may have been a suicide hotline, but in many ways we were like any other office. We complained about people not refilling the coffee, which brewed 24/7 along with the hotline operations. We dealt with passive-aggressive e-mails from management. Certain employees were the go-to people to refill the water cooler because others weren't strong enough – and I'll have you know I did that shit in heels no less. And we had a food thief.

I don't know what it is about an office setting that seems to embolden people to steal from others, but it seems everyone I know who's worked in an office has had to deal with a food thief. What's funny about it is every day those of us who answered the information lines – pretty much everyone who wasn't brand new – looked up information as to where needy people could get food. Someone, probably Kathi or Meeke, even put a sign on the fridge: "Please only eat the food you have brought in. If you are struggling to get food, please see management privately to discuss options." One would think that if you truly believe people are stealing out of need rather than selfishness, maybe you should raise your employees' salaries.

Most of us fell prey to the food thief at some point or other. Suspicions were whispered, mainly against the overnight people since there were fewer people working and thus less chance of getting caught, but there was never any proof. We'd swear, vent a moment, then forage for what sustenance could be found in the vending machine.

Then Zelda's food was stolen.

"No!" she shouted. All of us heard her, and a few people on the phone heard her too. "This did not just happen to me!"

We all thought this would be the end of it – we'd all had our food stolen, after all. But this was not the end for Zelda. She sent out an e-mail to everyone on all shifts, denouncing the food thief and ending with "Thou shalt not steal." She went through the fridge for any food she'd left in there: several people kept bottles of condiments for take-out. She had already labeled them all with her name and a cute heart. Now she added the note "DO NOT STEAL!" on every one of them. Others followed her lead.

I could only laugh. Would that really cow the food thief into proper behavior? Of course it didn't. Food went missing the very next day. It went on as it had for a time until Zelda had her food stolen again.

Now her notes were different. Along with her name and the commandment "DO NOT STEAL!" there was the addendum "I spit in it."

"I did too, for real," she'd tell those of us who asked her about it. "I don't even care."

Around this time all of us had ordered out. By the way, that's a fun thing, ordering food when you work in a locked building. Hopefully the delivery guy isn't one of the "bad crazies," I guess. Anyway, I had some leftovers I was going to store in the fridge. The white Styrofoam of the container yawned in front of me like a blank canvas. I wrote my name in big, sloppy letters. Then I added:

"Do not steal, look at, or think about. In fact, stop reading this!"

The food thief passed me over. Zelda gave me a fist-bump.

Brief (Non) Diversion and Becoming Queen

Kathi is leaving the company. I think this means Meeke will be the only one in charge. It's a fair theory since we go to her for most of our questions already anyway. But no: We have a new head honcho. Her name is Leann. If Kathi was distant, Leann is interplanetary, just as cold, just as hard to reach. I don't see that much good will come of this changing of the guard. Neither does Angelica: She retires, leaving us short a shift supervisor. That's when Maggie and Sam approach me.

I'm flattered, but surprised. I'm one of the youngest workers there, if not the youngest. I've long since learned that my Bachelor's is little more than an expensive piece of paper, that plenty of people with less education than me can do just as good a job. But I have been in grad school for a little while now, which I hope speaks for something. I happily take the promotion and the slight increase in pay that it brings.

In my personal life, I find myself drawn to a friend of Mike's. The walls of my resolve to stay away from men are crumbling. Sadly, this man has no interest in me. I've allowed my protections to fall, and I'm feeling lonelier than ever. It's a good thing I've been assigned as supervisor for Friday and Saturday nights: I have nowhere better to be anyway.

I've been starting to burn out a little lately between going to grad school part-time (the only way I can afford it) and working full-time. Forty hours a week of listening to people in need does take its toll, but I know that the jobs open to me without the Master's are not ones that interest me. I think that becoming a supervisor will offer me a new satisfaction that I've lacked in all other parts of my life. Instead it adds a whole new layer of weird to things.

Meetings are an exercise in patience and the virtues of silence. The more I speak out, the longer they last. And it seems, the more we talk about, the less gets accomplished. Every time, I'm reminded of the scene in *The Music Man* where the ladies are all gossiping, looking and sounding like a bunch of angry chickens. I'm often simply talked over anyway, being both the youngest and newest shift supervisor. This also means I get stuck with most of the holiday shifts, since "you don't have a family," as if having children was the only way to legitimately expect time for the holidays.

Additionally, without meaning to, I have become the queen of the passive aggressive e-mail. Every office has to deal with those e-mails from management, the "friendly reminders" to keep in line. My supervisors have noticed my skills in note-writing, and so have put me in charge of these e-mails.

I can feel the rest of the staff loathing me from a distance, and I know these e-mails are why. I don't mind really. There are people here I like, but no one here who I'd count as a true friend. Up until now I've always been in the corner-cube, minding my own business, and even though now I'm in The Big Girl Chair, I'm still just as distant. I retreat to books during my breaks.

Meeke is always interested in what I'm reading. Sometimes she'll sneak up behind me and start reading over my shoulder. She always apologizes, but it doesn't stop her from doing it again, even if it's a text book for school. I like Meeke. She's smart and skilled and snarky when she thinks she can get away with it. Like me, she's pale and plus-sized, but unlike me she dresses stylishly, always looking effortless in her business-casual. She's probably only ten years my senior, but I can't help but think of her as the sort of person I want to be when I grow up.

Under the Gun

The phone rings. There is no phone number on my screen. I answer.

"Hi… I heard this is a safe place to talk about suicide."

Nothing like jumping in with both feet. I confirm it is.

"Well… I'm in my car. Don't try to find me. I have a gun. I guess I just want to talk to someone to figure out why I shouldn't use it."

This is not a new request, but it's also not a fair one. Why would you call strangers and ask them to tell you why you shouldn't kill yourself? You're going to get a lot of vague answers, nothing personalized to your life: Life gets better, nothing can be that bad, what about your friends and family, maybe there's a hell, etc. If you're really thinking about suicide and need a reason not to do it, ask your friends. You'll get a helluva more helpful response from someone who knows you well than from a random stranger on the phone, no matter how well-meaning they are.

Still, the guy was suicidal. And worse, he had a gun. It's bad enough when someone has already opened their wrists or thrown back a load of sleeping pills, but those are usually easy to recover from, as a rule. A well-placed bullet pretty well puts an end to any sort of negotiations. "Working under the gun" has a whole new world of meaning when you work in this business.

I answer his request the way I usually do. "I want to give you reasons to hold on. It might be easier if I knew what's going on for you, what's making you feel like suicide is an option for you." That way the door is left open for him to talk about whatever he needs to talk about, so he can work it out for himself.

He takes my opening and runs with it. First he asks me not to laugh, and I worry that maybe I have a sex caller after all. But no –

"When I was a kid, I had a babysitter mess with me. A lot. And no one ever believed me because they said a boy can't get raped."

I'm not laughing, and I tell him so. At that moment, I can't think of anything less funny. I asked him if he's ever gotten any help for this – clearly it's still affecting him, not just that he was violated but that no one ever believed him. He says he hasn't. I ask him if he'd be willing to tell me where he's located – just the city, not where he is right now – so I can try to find resources for him. Thankfully, he agrees. Even more mercifully, he lives in a city about an hour away, one we have a little information about.

Our luck continues: I find a resource for him that has a sexual assault support group. As I've been looking all this up, he and I have been talking. Mainly I've been supporting him, applauding his courage for reaching out today rather than just acting on his suicidal thoughts, for disclosing his sexual abuse even though he's had such a bad response in the past. We have a pretty good rapport at this point, so he agrees to stay on hold while I call the agency I've found to verify they'd help him. They say they have a support group once a week specifically for men, as well as individual counseling.

I return back to the caller and tell him all this. I offer to connect him to the agency. He declines, but he asks for their phone number. He says he needs to calm down a bit before he calls them on his own, which he promises to do. I know that anyone can make any promises they want when they're on the phone with me, but words in this world are not as cheap as they are in most offices. They're all we have.

He tells me he's put his gun in the glove compartment. That the gun is away, and it's going to stay that way. I believe him. He tells me I've truly saved a life today, thanks me, and hangs up.

I take a deep breath. I finish my notes. I return my phone to the Ready position, and I wait for another call.

Lesson: You really can talk your way out of anything.

Diversion – Grad School

You might not think of working towards your Master's degree as a diversion, but when you spend all week listening to various crises as calmly as possible, burying yourself in books – even dry, clinical ones – is a welcome distraction. I'll read the entire section on personality disorders in the *DSM-IV-TR*, then the most up-to-date tome of psych disorders; just give me a break from *listening to* all these terrible things.

My graduate degree will be in mental health counseling, which will make me a mental health counselor. We get better training than social workers about diagnoses and treatment, but social workers have the benefit of having been recognized as a "real" profession for longer, so it makes it a little harder for people with my degree to get hired. I don't know that yet, as I'm not looking for a new job right now.

Here's a fun fact about graduate school, or at least the one I'm going to: Our training in suicide prevention is woefully inadequate. We spend maybe an hour and a half max on the topic, the same topic I've spent multiple hours on at the hotline. There are people with GEDs working at the hotline that have more training in suicide prevention than these people studying for their Master's. I am often the one who volunteers for projects on the topic, recognizing myself as the expert in the room, a first for me. With permission, I use the training material from the hotline rather than the skimpy resources in our texts. I start to call myself Suicide Sue in my head.

I look around my classes more than once at these classmates of mine with all kinds of varying skills and experience. Some have worked with developmentally delayed adults, incarcerated men, battered women, emotionally disturbed children, folks with substance abuse disorders – all populations that could be at risk for suicide. My classmates all have different strengths – empathy, acceptance, resiliency in the face of hardship – but looking around, I can't help but think to myself, *If I was suicidal again, I wouldn't trust any of these fuckers to talk me down.*

Side track from our story for a moment: While I was in graduate school, at the hotline we began implementing a new training mandatory for all of us, even those who had already attended Meeke's workshops on Mental Health 101 and Suicide Studies. The training is called ASIST: Applied Suicide Intervention Skills Training. That's its real name, you can look it up. It's a two-day intensive training that can be utilized by anyone who wants the training, not just people working at crisis hotlines. It would probably be best utilized by those who work with the public that might encounter crises: police, members of clergy, teachers, doctors/nurses – and mental health professionals.

After sitting through the two days, I raved about it to my professors and classmates, trying to finally get them interested in suicide prevention. I recommended they all try to get the training, by hook or by crook. They laughed me off – oh, Suicide Sue is harping on about suicide prevention again! It infuriated me. I already knew more about suicide prevention from those two full-time days than they did from their two full-time years in school. How I loathed them. Well, see how they react the first time they have a suicidal client, then we'll see who's laughing.

Anyone reading this who works with the public in the professions I just mentioned, or anyone who wants to know more about suicide prevention: All kidding aside, I can't recommend this training enough. It is, in my opinion, the best way to introduce suicide prevention to those who want to help but don't know how. A mental health background is not necessary, though it doesn't hurt either. As of my writing this, it's become more prevalent in the US (it began in Canada), even branching out into a few schools, as the training is meant for anyone 16 or over. If this is something that interests you remotely, please look for a session in your area. As of publication, you can do that by going to: https://www.livingworks.net/programs/asist/

Lucky Penny

The voice on the other end is more of a grumble than speech. "Yeah, so I heard I could talk here."

"That's right."

"Yeah. Well, I guess I'm at the end of my rope. That's a fitting thing to say. I have a rope here. Not that I'd use it. It might not work; I could end up even more of a problem. I'd probably use the gun downstairs. Quicker that way."

"So it sounds like you're thinking of suicide."

This might seem like a dumb thing to say, but part of our jobs is to clarify the caller's state of mind, and that might involve saying the S-word out loud where they won't. It helps to make sure we have all the cards on the table, so to speak.

The caller snorts. "Yeah, you could say that. And I'm just trying to reach out in case maybe there's another way."

"OK. Let's talk. My name is Penny, can I ask yours?"

He snorts again. "Just call me Joe. I'm not giving you my real name."

"That's fine. We can just talk." Really it is. I like to try getting on a first-name basis with my callers to encourage us connecting, but it's not required or anything. It is nice to know who you're actually talking with, so I try to make a point to introduce myself, especially if the person on the line is the one who's at risk.

The caller seems to relax at the fact that I'm not demanding anything of him. He explodes with his story:

He says he's a drunk. Alcoholics go to meetings, and he hasn't been to one in months, so he supposes that means he's a drunk. He's intoxicated tonight; this actually surprises me, since usually slurring gives it away, but he's speaking clearly. His drinking drove his wife away. She took their baby with her. He weeps when he speaks about his son, clearly quite proud as he declares, "That's my *boy*." On top of all this, his business that he's spent years building is on the verge of collapse. He can't help but wonder if it would be better for everyone involved if he simply wasn't there anymore. By now he is sloppily crying into the phone and we've been talking for about an hour.

"So I guess that's why I called tonight, Penny," he whimpers. "I don't really want to die but I feel like that would help everyone. Including me…" He breaks off into a choking sob.

I'm quiet a little while, letting him collect himself. "That's so much going on. I understand why you'd think suicide was an option open to you."

Again, this may seem like a dumb thing to say. But it's actually not. Suicidologists suggest that it can be helpful to acknowledge why a person might feel suicidal because it normalizes their feelings. *Then* you can bring it back to why a person would want to live.

"I wonder," I muse aloud, "We've been talking a while. I wonder if you'd be OK with letting me know where you are so I could see if I have information for your area."

Given how reluctant he was at first, I could see him rejecting me. But as I say, we have been talking for about an hour now. It feels like he knows he can trust me at this point.

My bet has paid off. "Yeah. Yeah, Penny, can you do that for me?"

"Yeah, Joe. I can."

"No," he says, "You don't have to call me that now. It's really Terry. Terry Acevedo." He tells me the city he's in.

"All right, Terry. It's Saturday night, so no counselor or anything is going to be open. But what about trying to make it to AA tomorrow? You said you've been before."

He sniffles a little. "I could try that. I think I know where the closest meeting is."

I'm already pulling up the AA website. "Well, let's see the closest meeting for tomorrow. I'm worried about keeping you safe, so I want the soonest thing we can find for you." That's how I tend to phrase things: *I'm worried* and *I want to keep you safe*. It's true for one thing, but also it can help put things back on the caller: by keeping themselves safe, they're doing a favor to the telecounselor, with whom they've (hopefully) connected.

We find an AA meeting not too far from him that takes place Sunday night. I express my concern that he might still be tempted to act on his suicidal thoughts before the meeting. I ask if there's anyone who can hold on to the key to his gun cabinet, just for a little while. He sheepishly admits there's no lock on it. This always makes me scream inside, especially when there are kids. I have nothing against people owning guns, but they should be kept safely locked up; access to a gun has been shown to increase the risk of suicide, especially in young people.

"Honestly," he says, "I'm feeling a lot calmer now that we've talked. I don't feel like reaching for that gun or rope or anything. For the first time in a long time, I feel like I have hope to turn things around."

If we hadn't been talking as long as we had, I'd probably think he was bullshitting me. But as I've said before, words are the only currency we have to trade in on the hotline, and we've spent over an hour building trust between us. Yes, that goes both ways: He trusts me enough to allow me to help him, but also I trust him enough that he'll hold true to his word and won't kill himself after we've hung up.

"OK," I say. "I'm going to trust you that you're going to be safe, at least until that AA meeting tomorrow. And if that changes, you'll call back?"

"I will, Penny."

"Even if that changes in just a few minutes or a few hours? You'll call back to make a new safety plan?"

"Yes. I promise." He says it fervently, like it's a sacred vow.

Since we've got an understanding between us, I add something I don't always add. "You can talk to anybody here like you would talk to me. If you want, you can tell them you talked to me, but everybody here is here to help you."

This might seem vain or just odd, but there's a reason I throw this in. Sometimes callers get really connected to that one person that they get on the line. Some even think that person becomes "their counselor." We've been talking so long, it's possible Terry thinks I'm the only one able to assist him – after all, he himself said I'm the first person in a long time who he's felt has helped him. So I want to make it perfectly clear that we all have the same training, and anyone can help him make a plan to keep safe. I might have my personal opinions as to who does it better, but he doesn't need to know that.

"Penny," he sighs, "My dear. I can honestly say you have saved a life tonight. You've been such a sweetheart. My dear."

I worry he might be getting too close, so I laugh, "Oh Terry, I bet you tell all the telecounselors that!"

Thankfully, he laughs too. "But seriously, I mean it, Penny. You've been so sweet. I won't forget tonight. Thank you so much. Thank you for taking the time to talk to a miserable bum and giving him some hope for a change. I mean that."

I'm smiling, and probably blushing. Even if you get thanked daily, it's rarely so effusive. "You're welcome, Terry. And remember that we're here if you need to call back any time."

"I will. My dear. Thank you."

The call ends. I stretch out, worn out from this marathon call. I feel genuinely good about how the call ended as I type up my notes and go on with my night. I end my evening thinking to myself I made a difference, at least to that one caller who had started out so gruff. Soon it's gone from my mind and I don't think of Terry again.

Then he calls back. It's Tuesday. Again, he's more grumbling than speaking.

"Yeah. Yeah, I guess this is it. There's nothing left. Y'know, you work all your life and what does it get you? Nothing."

This is where our database comes in handy: I see his phone number on the call ID and look him up – we talk to people all day, after all, and sometimes you don't recognize every voice you hear, even ones with whom you spend hours. A quick search pulled up my previous call.

"I called here before, actually," he's going on, "And here I am again."

"Actually," I pipe in gently. "I'm the one you talked to before. I'm Penny."

He gasps. "Penny!" He says it like recognizing an old lover, fondly, genuine in his surprise.

"Yes, Terry," I say, reminded of his name from my database search, "It's me."

"Oh, Penny. Sweetheart."

It legitimately is luck that he's reached my phone again. Certain numbers don't route to certain telecounselors or anything, as much as it may feel like that to us some days. Callers reach the person who's been without a call the longest. I'm grateful for the coincidence since it gives me a natural leg-up in understanding him: I've already talked to him for over an hour, and it wasn't that long ago, so I understand him a little better than someone going in blind.

"Terry, we made that plan a few days ago. How did it work out for you?"

Well, not so great, it turns out. He tried to go to the AA meeting, as was agreed, but for reasons unknown, they cancelled, and the next meeting in his area was days away. Left with nothing to do and no other help on a Sunday night, he got drunk again. He went to work hungover, trying to scrape together the fraying ends of his business, but received more bad news that made it seem less likely he could recover. Then earlier today he finally heard from his wife: She's not only filing for divorce, she's also filing for sole custody of their son, the child in whom he takes so much pride. Again, he's a mess of tears.

"I could take her leaving," he blubbers, "As much as I still love her, I've known for a while our relationship was ending. But *my boy*… To take my little boy…" He dissolves into sniffling.

My heart really goes out to this guy. No, he's not innocent in this – he's the one who drove his wife to what she's doing with his drinking – but I have to hand it to him that he really is trying to stick around for his son. He says that's the main reason he hasn't already shot himself: "I figure a drunk, broke dad is better than no dad… But sometimes it's more the fact that I know they wouldn't get my life insurance if I offed myself."

"Honestly, even if that's all that's keeping you here, that's something," I admit, "And I think you really know, deep down, you need to be there for your son." I don't usually like to hold guilt like that over a person – *you need to stick around for your family* – but I'm increasingly worried about how little is holding him back from suicide.

"I do, Penny, I do!" he exclaims hurriedly.

"I know. So we have to figure out a new plan to keep you safe." Again, *we*. This is a team effort.

A second time, we've been talking nearly an hour by now. It takes us a bit of brainstorming, but together we come up with an idea to keep him safe: It's getting late tonight, so he will go to bed. Tomorrow he will call his lawyer to sort out the divorce and custody proceedings. After that he'll call his health insurance company to find a counselor that accepts his insurance. The next AA meeting in his town isn't until tomorrow, but he'll go to that. And there's always the hotline again, if anything comes up.

"I know I said it before, Penny," Terry says, calm once again. "but I really feel hopeful. I messed up before, but I'm not going to do that again."

"You're allowed to mess up," I correct him, "as long as you stay safe."

"I'm safe," he insists, and I believe him. "I'm safe to go through with our plan. Penny. My sweetheart. You've been so good to me. I don't know how to thank you. I'm so happy I got you again tonight."

"I'm glad, too. I don't know whatever sent you to my phone again tonight, but I'm glad." But I remind him, "If you need to call again, chances are you'll get someone else. And they'll be happy to talk to you and help you too. Anyone here will be glad to rework your safety plan until you feel you can be safe."

"I know I'll be safe. Thanks to you. Penny. Oh, my dear Penny. There are no words I can use to thank you enough."

Before when he thanked me I was grinning. Now I'm almost embarrassed by his enthusiasm. "It's nothing, Terry. I'm glad to do it." I mean this. As much as I may complain about my job, and as stressful as it can be, I am genuinely glad to help draw people back from the depths of their despair. It confirms that saving myself those years ago was a good decision.

"Penny. Thank you."

"You're welcome, Terry. And you have a good night."

"I will now." Then he adds, as earnestly as a prayer, "Good night, my love."

He hangs up, but I know what I heard. I shake my head and type up my notes. The overnight shift supervisor, Rose, has just come in, and I tell her what just happened, especially the last thing Terry said. She chuckles. Again, I finish up my shift and don't think of Terry again.

Until I come in a few days later.

No, I didn't get him a third time – though that would be some serious machinations by Fate to have me get him again in that many calls. No, Rose came in again to relieve me.

"Penny!" she smiles. "Your friend Terry called again last night."

Again, I can't remember the name and voice of everyone I talk to, so at first I'm clueless. But I think a bit and it comes to me. "Oh! Is he OK?" That's always the first reaction in this business.

"You certainly made an impression on him, Miss Penny."

"Uh-oh."

"Well, he didn't like what I had to say." I remember how he had started out tough in both of my calls with him. "Then finally he shouted at me, over and over, 'I want to talk to Penny!'"

That's a strict no-no with us: Whoever you get when the phone rings is the person you talk to. It doesn't matter if you've called before and really got along with one telecounselor or really didn't like another; who you get is who you get. And now despite all my reassurances that anyone else could help him, this caller is convinced I'm his personal savior. Great.

Lesson: Even in this business, sometimes it really is possible to do your job *too* well.

The Saga of Sam and Vena

Sam has been dating her girlfriend Vena for longer than I've worked there, but since I got hired it seemed clear they didn't have the best relationship. They were always tumultuous, on-again, off-again. One week Sam would be glowing with pride about how "beautiful" and "wonderful" Vena was, the next she'd be cursing women. I just shook my head. My relationships had certainly never been perfect, but I guess I just didn't see the appeal to constant turmoil in one's love life.

Things looked like they were going much as they had for the past few years, but the mood became decidedly darker around Sam and Vena's downward swings. Vena would call the hotline's supervisor phone, and as soon as Sam was on the line, she'd start screaming. Sam would buy Vena a new pair of diamond earrings. Sam came home one day to find her possessions had all been put into garbage bags, which Vena was dragging to the curb. Sam would buy her a designer purse. Vena had cracked several of Sam's video games. Sam got Vena's name tattooed on her arm.

"I already got it planned out," she said, pointing to the reddened flesh, "If we break up I can change it to Virgo 'cause that's my birth sign."

I decided not to voice my opinion that if you're already planning the cover-up, maybe you shouldn't have gone ahead with the tattoo.

These incidents with Vena became more and more frequent. It came to be that Sam spent more time on the phone with Vena on her shifts than she did with callers. And since Sam was technically my supervisor, I couldn't say or do anything about it. I tried talking to Meeke once, as I knew she'd be more helpful than Leann.

"Yeaahhhhhhh," she drawled, "Sam's going through a rough time."

"I get that. But her rough time is starting to affect how we help people out there."

I knew that I was probably not being the most sensitive of coworkers at this moment. I knew quite well that while there may have never been blows, Vena was abusive. I knew that abused partners are at risk of losing their jobs because of their abuser's shenanigans. But despite knowing all this, I didn't care. As a shift supervisor, my job was to make sure everyone is doing their jobs right, and I couldn't manage up: Maybe I couldn't discipline Sam, but Meeke could.

Instead Sam got extra time off on the weekends to attend couples' counseling. Until she and Vena finally split for good. Nearly a whole year had gone by during all this.

Looking back, I should be grateful that I worked for a company that was that understanding to an abused partner that they allowed her some time to work through it. But at the time I was livid. Every time I got my grad school schedule, I had to rework my entire schedule, which would always make Maggie and Leann grimace and tut and tell me how hard it was, but Sam gets a crazy girlfriend, and she gets coddled? It felt so unfair.

Lesson: Life isn't fair, dumbass.

Diversion – Grant

It was the end of September, getting close to my birthday. I decided I wanted to go out to sushi with friends. However I found myself in the unenviable position of realizing that I didn't have many friends left. A lot had been mutual friends with Mike, all college students who had since graduated and left the city. A lot had been left by the wayside between grad school and working my strange schedule – some of them left me, but I did my fair share of leaving them. In my efforts to further my career and education, I'd completely forgotten about having friends with whom I could share my joy.

But I wasn't completely alone: There was Melody, whom I'd known since second grade, and her boyfriend Leo. I'd met Leo a few times, and he seemed a decent enough fellow. I could see them lasting a good long while. Leo said he had a guy friend who was single, maybe he could come along? It had been a long time since my last near-diversion, and one might think I'd be hesitant. Actually, I was relieved. Having one more person there would make it seem like I had more friends, and if it led to something more than friendship then that would be great. If not? Well, I think I finally had gathered enough confidence around myself that I could deal with that too.

I met the three of them at the sushi bar. Leo's friend, Grant, smiled politely and even pulled my chair out for me. The four of us mostly chit-chatted about idle topics, nothing really deep. I think both Grant and I were nervous, but maybe it was just me. I wanted this blind date – my first ever – to work out, but I wasn't really feeling anything. He was attractive enough, but I still didn't know anything about him except that he had been friends with Leo for many years. Still, as I say, I didn't mind if I just got another friend out of the deal.

Eventually we retreated from the sushi place and headed to Melody's place to hang out. I blared my music, VNV Nation, until the windows pulsed. I wondered if this music would become an unlikely reminder of a first date. We all arrived at the same time. Melody turned on the TV, and we mostly talked over it. Suddenly Grant's earlier reticence was gone, and he opened up. He was working tech support right now, but he didn't like it. He was thinking about going back to school – he had never gotten his Bachelor's. If you remember, I once held a Bachelor's as the bare minimum a person needed to succeed at life; although I knew better now, old beliefs die hard, and I asked why he never got his degree.

"Oh, I was in the Army."

This may not seem exotic to others, but to me the military was something you only did if you didn't have any other choice. I now see that's not a fair assumption, but at the time my only interaction with the Army was my paternal grandpa, who'd been drafted and wouldn't speak about his war experience; my maternal grandpa, who had gone to Korea a kid and came back a wife-beater; and some anti-war documentaries. Still, I did go to high school with a few people who went to West Point, so I had a little exposure to the military in a positive vein.

I kept my reaction light. "Oh?"

"Yeah, then they kicked me out."

Now I was baffled. They didn't just kick anybody out, did they? Coolly, I asked, "Can I ask, what happened?" That had become my *modus operandi* when on the phone inquiring about delicate subjects – ask permission to ask about something.

Grant was nonchalant. "Oh yeah. They caught me doing whippets."

I admit, it took me a minute to register what he even meant because I hadn't heard about whippets since high school sociology. Do people really get high that way? Like, outside of junior or senior high I mean. Even though I had no interest in it, I knew exactly how I could have gotten a hold of pot, which seemed a much healthier way of getting high, if there is such a thing.

Whippets. Goddamn.

I reached in to my telecounselor empathy and merely responded, "Oh, OK." Like that was the most normal thing in the world to do, and that anyone could get caught doing it and get discharged from the Army. *Of course.*

He nods appreciatively. "It was really dumb," he mumbles.

I simply shrug. I agree with him, but I don't want to say so.

We while away the time until it gets late and we all mutually agree we should hit the bricks. Grant approaches me. "Can I get your number?" he asks.

I appreciate he's not being coy. I give it to him, and he gives me his. I'm still not feeling attracted to him really – freakin' *whippets*, man – but I figure I'm up for giving him a chance.

I don't really think much about Grant for a while. I spend a week working my normal schedule. At one point on my break, Meeke catches me texting Melody. As usual, she asks about it.

"Oh. My friend tried to set me up with someone recently. I don't think it went very well, but we'll see."

"Oh, well," Meeke begins, glancing around to make sure we're alone, "If it doesn't work out – not that I'm wishing that for you – I think I know some people I could set you up with."

I'm surprised, but not unpleasantly so. I've always liked Meeke, and it shows she's thinking of me if she can think of some people to set me up with. "Really?"

She nods, glancing around again. "I actually have a roommate who lives with me and Joseph," she says referring to her boyfriend, "He's a great guy, though he's a bit clueless when it comes to women. But... Well, I don't know. Do you go for older guys?"

I tell her I don't know. I've actually never dated an older guy. We've always been the same age, give or take.

"Well..." She looks me up and down. "I'd say he's probably ten years older. Does that change your mind?"

I cringe a bit and nod. "I mean… I don't know. I feel like that much difference... It could get weird."

"That's OK!" she jumps in. "I have a buffet of nerds I can lay before you!"

I laugh, and I appreciate that she knows I'd work with a nerdy guy. Maybe it's the fact that I requested the day off when the last *Harry Potter* book came out. Or the time she saw me reading *Dune*. Or the movie references I've made in e-mails to her, or the times I've remembered Talk Like a Pirate Day, or any number of little quirks she's catalogued on me over the years.

She goes on. "I actually throw a Halloween party every year. Maybe you could come and meet some of them?"

I smile. "That would be awesome." Secretly, I am doing a little dance inside my head. I'm making friends with someone I've always admired, and through her I might make more friends. The rest of the day I'm beaming.

When I get home, I see that I've gotten a voicemail. It's from Grant. I listen.

"Hey, Penny. It's Grant. Um. IIIII was just thinking maybe we couldgooutsometime. Um. Yeah. Get back to me. IIIIII guess I'll talk to you soon."

I grin. Well, today was going well. I call Grant back, but I get his voicemail. I frown, but I'm upbeat on my message. "Hey Grant, it's Penny. I got your message. Yeah, going out sounds great. I'm working Friday and Saturday, but maybe we could get coffee or something Sunday? Anyway, I'll talk to you later."

I feel good about it until I get another voicemail from Grant a few days later.

"Heeeeyyyyyy. Penny. I actually don't remember calling you before. I think I was a little drunk. But yeah, let's go out some time. I'll talk to you later."

I look at my cell and snort in disbelief. First whippets, now getting blackout drunk. No. If I was getting back in the saddle, I wasn't doing it with anyone's baggage but my own.

The next day I pulled Meeke aside. "Yeah. It totally didn't work with that other guy. I'd like to see what's on the buffet."

Diversion – Grant 2.0

That semester I was taking an extra class, one on substance abuse counseling. I thought it might help me graduate early, but really it just gave me more added stress. I was snappy at everybody from lack of sleep and free time. It was just as well I didn't have that many friends, as it's sheer good fortune I didn't drive away the ones I had left.

Meeke called me into her office one day when it was slow. She had me shut the door behind me, which was odd.

"So I talked to my friends," she said. "We do a sort of weekly dinner club – nothing fancy, just a dish to pass and some wine. I told them I'd invited you to the Halloween party, but they were so excited to hear about you, they said you should come to dinner club. So yeah, if you're free Friday after work, you're totally invited."

I tried not to show how excited I was. "That would be great!"

She handed me a print-out of directions how to get from the hotline to her house. "How about you bring those chocolate chip cookies you're always bringing in on the weekend?" She winks.

It was true: Any time there was a potluck, I'd bring my usual cookies– just the Tollhouse recipe with a little extra vanilla – but I always brought more on the weekend. I figure we're already screwed having to work times when our families had off, we may as well eat good food.

Then she adds "Oh, and bring a bottle of wine. We're a bunch of lushes. Oh. And this should be implied, what with the closed door and everything, but don't tell anyone. I don't want it getting out I'm pally with some people and not others." She sends me back to my desk just as if this was a business meeting.

I fold the directions up and put them in my pocket. They sit there, hot in my khakis, like a secret note you're passed in class. When I leave, I see that Meeke doesn't live all that far from the hotline. I wonder if she ever feels like she can get away. At this time, I'm still living with my parents, so I know that feeling. Nothing against them or anything, but when you have superiors at work and elders at home, a young adult starts to feeling like she doesn't really have a place in the world.

Thursday night I make cookies while studying the stages of recovery. I try not to eat as much cookie dough as I normally would because I want there to be plenty for these people I'm trying to woo as my friends. I remember that Meeke mentioned a roommate she'd initially thought would be a good match for me. I suppose he'll be there. I wonder if it will be weird.

Here's something I've since learned about that Friday night meeting: It was arranged a little bit differently than Meeke initially described to me.

While Meeke was telling me about her "buffet of nerds," she was also telling her dinner club about me, which I knew. What I didn't know was the roommate she spoke of piped in. "You can't just wait for Halloween," he protested. "What if I like her? Then there will be all these other guys there, and you know I'm no good with that. Invite her to dinner club first. That way, if I like her, I can get my name in early."

To an outsider, that might come off as arrogant. But would it help you to know I ended up with that guy? To me, it's actually really cute.

I made two batches of cookies. Meeke's request to bring wine actually baffled me: All my alcoholic experience had been classless mixed drinks and shots, nothing with a hint of respectability like wine. I was glad she'd mentioned labels they usually drank because I knew what to look for at the liquor store. Since I didn't know the difference between white and red, I compromised and got a huge bottle of rose. The attendees declared it a victory, if for no reason other than the sheer volume I brought.

There was a total of eight, myself included. Meeke's and Joseph's roommate, it turned out, was also named Grant. Who knew it was such a popular name? With the exception of Grant and me, everyone was a part of a couple. I don't even remember what we first said to each other, but it was clear we were both interested. He's tall, of average to large build, and has cornflower blue eyes.

After dinner, we retreated to the living room for a movie. There was only so much seating, so Grant and I were stuck sitting on the brand new dog bed meant for Meeke and Joseph's newly adopted German shepherd. Initially we sat a respectable distance from each other, until the dog decided he'd had enough of being patient with people in his bed and plopped down next to me, shoving me next to Grant. Eventually I felt a casual arm around my shoulder. Outwardly I was calm and cool, but inwardly I was exploding with excitement.

The movie ends. As time goes on people begin to get tired, then finally excuse themselves. Even Meeke and Joseph go upstairs to bed while Grant and I stay up talking about everything, and even sometimes just quietly watching TV together. By and by it gets to be two in the morning, and I figure I should get to sleep, which means getting on the road to head home.

We linger on the front porch, saying our goodbyes. There's a slight awkward silence before finally Grant asks "Can I give you my number?"

I smile at the way he's phrased it. That way if I wasn't interested, I could always decline. But I'm very interested, and I pull out my phone. The first Grant's phone number is still in there, the one who called me while blackout drunk. I haven't deleted it yet. I ask this much cooler Grant his last initial. It's O. I have him saved in my phone, "Grant O yes!," and I tell him my number, which I watch him enter into his phone. We are awkward at the door a bit longer, and I go to my car.

While I'm driving home, I feel my cell phone vibrate, indicating I've gotten a text message. I know I shouldn't, but at a stop light I read it. It's from "Grant O yes!"

I'm so dumb. I should have kissed you good night.

I let out a squeal. I wait till I get home to reply. *There will be time for that.* ☺ I worry I'm being too forward, but something just feels right with him.

My feeling is right: He texts the next day and asks if I would like to join him out. I realize I suddenly hate my schedule, which has me working Saturday nights, and I tell him so. *But I'm free tomorrow after 8?* Normally I'd be free all night, but for my substance abuse class, I need to attend a twelve-step meeting, and the one I plan on going to is tomorrow at 7. Ironically, we agree to meet at a pub that has a trivia night.

When I arrive, he's already there. I laugh, "Guess where I just came from? An AA meeting!" I figure if he doesn't see the humor in this, even after I explain it, then maybe he's not the one for me. But thankfully, he does. We're both miserable at the trivia, only getting two or three right out of twenty, but we have a good time anyway. He walks me to my car, where he kisses me. We're both awkward, but it still feels right. I nursed a single hard cider the whole night and then switched to water, but I'm still feeling light-headed as I drive home.

We text each other all week. We meet at a restaurant in the mall for a date. Afterwards we're going to go shopping for pieces for our Halloween costumes. I've been enjoying the ride so far, but I finally have to let out what's been on my mind.

"I'm going to grad school right now."

"I remember," he tells me.

"Yeah, but I'm taking three classes. That might not sound like a lot, but that's more than I'm used to. And I'm working full-time. I only got promoted not that long ago. And Meeke can tell you I have a weird schedule."

"Yeah, she mentioned that."

"I don't know what I'm doing after graduation," I go on, my voice rising, "I've thought about getting my doctorate out of state, but I don't know. But even before that, while I'm still in grad school, I'm going to need to do two internships. So, like, I'd be taking a class, and basically working two jobs. So… You just need to know that. Sometimes now, and also coming up my schedule is going to be crazy."

I know I've just ruined this lovely little bud of a romance. I've crushed it with my anxiety, or maybe with my ambition. This guy is going to know how messed up I really am.

Instead he reaches across the table and holds my hand gently. "I guess we'll have to figure that out together," he shrugs.

Five months later, we had moved in together.

Penny v. Jenna

Everyone has stylistic differences when it comes to approaching calls. I'll admit, I tend towards the touchy-feely because that's just the sort of person I am. Other people are more matter-of-fact because that's how they are. As long as they aren't actually rude or hurtful to callers, then they get a pass.

Jenna was always just on that razor's edge between appropriate and not. She always sounded exhausted on her calls, like she was doing you a favor by answering calls that day and you better be grateful for it. She'd sigh like she was bored – which she probably was. She had this tone of voice that I couldn't describe as anything but snide. She was never really nasty, but she was often brusque, a curtness that I never felt was right given our line of work.

You might remember me saying I didn't like Jenna. Well, after a while it became clear she didn't like me either. Normally this would just be an inconvenience in the office, but when I got promoted, it came to a head. Jenna was put under my direct supervision, which meant I had a say in her performance review. You might think I relished the chance to really express how I felt about her, but it was actually the opposite: I knew I didn't like her, and I was afraid that my lack of objectivity in my feelings about her might become evident in my reviews. I didn't want to be *that* supervisor.

I tried to make it a point to look for her good behaviors, her admirable traits. I became distressed to learn I couldn't find too many. She loved her nieces and nephews, and she was doting to her pets, which counted for something, but it had nothing to do with her performance. I then made it a point not to put anything negative unless it really needed work. I relied heavily on input from other supervisors to make up her performance reviews.

As a shift supervisor, we often listened in on others' calls. This was so we could perform quality control in lieu of recording calls, which you'll remember we didn't do. If someone was struggling, they could ask a supervisor to listen in, or sometimes you could just call out something to someone who wasn't yet ready to admit she needed help.

One day it was getting towards the end of Jenna's shift. She was on a call with a frequent flyer who didn't have a policy limiting her calls. This caller was in the middle of what was a crisis to her, but to most people would just be an everyday hassle, nothing major. But to this caller it was a big fucking deal. In our training – the training I took with Jenna – we are told that even though something might seem laughable to us, we are never to belittle the caller's feelings. Well, listening to Jenna handle this call, I knew she didn't give a rat's ass, and the caller knew it too. The caller expressed that she felt she wasn't being respected.

"Well then," Jenna snapped, "you don't have to stay on this call." And she hung up.

Now, if we're being actively abused, pranked, or jerked off to, we are free to get off the line without any repercussions. But that wasn't the case here. Jenna was being a dick, she was called out on being a dick, and she dicked out even more by hanging up on the caller. And as a shift supervisor, it was my job to stop dickishness.

Normally if I had a major concern about a telecounselor's performance, I'd ask to see her in private to talk to her about it. But I knew Jenna. In her mind, she was always right. So I decided to write her an e-mail instead. It was our policy at the hotline to always have e-mail open all day, so I knew she would see it. I don't remember what all I said, because in keeping with my normal way of doing things, I was pretty wordy. Basically, it boiled down to something like this:

Jenna, I just listened to your call with Repeater Fay. She was distressed and seeking reassurance. Your response to her was very blasé and not very reassuring. Even though something may not seem like a crisis to us, it was a crisis to her, and it was not treated with the respect she should expect from us. The way the call was terminated was also unacceptable.

We loved the word "unacceptable" at the hotline. Don't ask me why.

I know it can be hard to hear criticism of ourselves, but you had the option of turning the call over to a supervisor (me or Marisol).

Both of us were working that day.

You are capable of great calls. In the future please remember to treat every crisis – even the ones that may seem silly to us – with the respect it deserves.

I know that looks pretty lengthy as it is, but I know it was longer. I wanted to be gentle, but still stress to her that her behavior was, in short, not cool. I sent it. I heard the bleep of a new e-mail on her computer, and I held my breath. Shortly thereafter Jenna was on her feet, and whirling by my desk.

"We need to talk," she hissed, continuing to walk by me. I got up and followed her. There was an unused room next to Meeke's office, one that was often used for supervisor-minion powwows like this, so I knew that was where she was heading. Sure enough, she was already in the room when I entered. I closed the door behind me for privacy's sake.

"What's on your mind?" I simpered.

She was already turning red. "You know what. That e-mail. I think it's crap."

I can honestly say I was surprised. Not so much that the e-mail had pissed her off, but the fact that she was bringing it up with me. I figured she'd send an e-mail about me to Sunny or someone else bitching about me behind my back – that was pretty much in line with her usual way of dealing with me. You know when people talk about you, and she did it plenty.

"I was concerned about the call," I replied in a voice calmer than how I felt, "I've heard you do better on other calls – ”

“I thought I did fine,” she interrupted me.

“Well, I listened in, and I disagreed.”

“What? Because I wasn’t like” – here her voice took on a piteous mewl – “*Oh poor baby!* like *you* would do?”

Her temper is making me more and more uncomfortable. Her volume has been raising and she’s been slowly getting closer to me. I know she won’t hit me – will she? – but it unnerves me nevertheless.

“We all have our different styles,” I breathe slowly, “And I can’t critique you just because you have a different style than me, But like I said, I’ve heard you do better on other calls – ”

“I think this is about something else,” she insists.

I know what she’s getting at, but I ask, “What’s that?”

“Don’t be stupid, you know exactly what.” She never comes right out and says *You don’t like me*, but it’s there, hanging sharp as the sword of Damocles.

“I really don’t know,” I lie, “To me this is about one call that I heard.”

“I’m going to talk to Marisol and Sam about this,” she retorts.

“That’s fine. That’s your right.” It really is. They’ll hear all about this from me too.

“And until they tell me otherwise, I’m going to do exactly what I have been doing on my calls.”

This catches me. She may not like me, she may not like what I have to say, but I’m still her supervisor.

Still, I’m too anxious to think of this. I just say the first thing that comes to me. “Well. I guess this meeting is over then.”

I open the door for her. She fumes out, goes back to her desk, logs out, and leaves in a storm cloud of fury.

I start to go back to my desk. Meeke peeps her head in and waves me towards her. I follow her to her office.

“I just heard all of that,” she gasps. “Dude. You and Jenna.”

I can’t help but blurt, “Did I handle that all right?”

“OK, so I didn’t hear all of it. I mainly heard Jenna yelling at you. What happened? A call?”

I summarize my version of events to her.

"OK. Yeah, maybe you should have talked to her instead of sending that e-mail but other than that? You handled it appropriately."

Meeke further instructs me to go to the file on the computer specifically for supervisors. She tells me to write, in detail, exactly what happened. She says she will write what she overheard. Later, after Jenna talks to them, Sam and Marisol add their testimony as to her behavior. Each of them state that Jenna indicated she wouldn't listen to what I said. And there it is again: refusal to listen to legitimate directions of a legitimate superior. This isn't just attitude, this is insubordination. People are fired for things like that.

Yeah, but not around here. We're too short of workers as it is to fire people for something as simple as not following directions. It's not like people's lives are on the line, right?

Jenna and I continue to work together. I'm sure she's just stewing in hate towards me, assuming she even gives me that much thought. I, meanwhile, have a gnawing anxiety eating at me. Normally I second-guess myself a lot, but in this situation I *know* I was right. When I ask what's to be done about this situation, everyone just shrugs. What does it say that I can't expect anything to be done about someone who, in my heart, I feel is actively doing harm to people in crisis?

Lesson: The squeaky wheel doesn't always get the attention.

A Natural Risk of the Business

The phone rings, I answer. I hear sniffling before anything else.

"H-Hello?" the voice sounds female, young, scared.

"Hi. This is the Crisis Hotline."

Some more sniffling.

"My name is Penny," I offer, "Can I ask your name?"

One more big sniff. "Um, yeah. I'm Caroline." She doesn't say anything more.

I get that sometimes people are unsure where to begin with calls like this. It's not exactly like calling mom on the holidays or anything. It's bound to be awkward if you're new to this sort of thing, which most people are. It all makes sense, but I can't help but feel like I'm pulling teeth on calls like this.

"Hi, Caroline. It sounds like you're pretty upset to be calling today."

Her voice squeaks out a broken, "Mm-hmm."

"What's got you so upset today?"

It takes her a few more sniffles before she can get going. I take the time to look up her phone number in the database. She has called a few times before, and skimming over the notes it looks like they were heavy suicides each time – never anything she'd actually done to harm herself, but it took a good deal of talking to keep her safe. I buckle in for a long haul.

I honestly don't remember why Caroline was suicidal, and in the end I suppose it doesn't really matter. The fact remains that she was, and severely so. There's something in her voice beneath the tears. It's a tone I recognize from my teenage years, that emptiness that barely shrouds a fundamentally broken interior. I have felt how she feels now: Hollow, fragile, and barely keeping it together. Even her sniffles I know are just leaks in the dam walling up her despair. She knows – I know – that if she lets too many leaks out, the terrible emotions will drown her. I don't say this about many of my callers, but I wish I could just hug her.

We talk for an hour, maybe longer. She agrees to my suggestion that she be seen by the urban hospital's mobile psychiatric team, an offshoot of their psychiatric emergency room. I figure maybe being seen by them will show her there is some hope. Or maybe they'll recommend hospitalization, which I think would likely help her. Something to break her out of her rut where she just dwells on the possibility of suicide. Since the referral goes through us at the hotline, I need to get off the phone to give the information to the team. I don't really feel like leaving Caroline alone, but I don't have any other option. I remind her she can call back if she feels unsafe.

There are some calls you get off of and you know for a fact you did a good job. This is the precise opposite: You get off feeling worse than you did when you started, unsure of yourself, seriously doubting the caller's safety. After I put in the referral to the team, I pull Maggie aside to talk about the call. She doesn't see that I could have done any differently.

"Oh Caroline?" John pipes in. "I had her a few days ago." He shakes his head. "She was a tough one. I'm glad she called back, because…" He doesn't finish the thought, but we all know what he means.

"Yeah," I gulp.

Days go by, then a week, then two. I come in for my evening shift. Maggie's brow is knit over her huge glasses.

"Penny, you got a minute?"

I have barely come in the door, of course I do. I plonk my purse down. "What's up?"

"Do you remember getting a call from a woman named Caroline?"

It takes me a while. Maggie begins to yammer a little about Caroline's stressors, and the call comes to me. "Oh yeah. What's up?"

"Well, you helped her get connected to the team, remember?" I nod. "Well, they went to see her again today, and…" Maggie's voice cracks a little. "Well, she had hanged herself."

I can't help it. I demand, "Was I the last person she talked to?"

"Oh no. She called back a couple of times, got Sunny and Laura – I've been able to tell them, and I'll be telling John when I see him Sunday. But since you were one of the people who made contact with her, we felt you should know."

"Thank you," I say automatically.

"The only reason we know is because you made that referral to the team, and they are so connected with us. Otherwise, we'd be in the dark."

Finally, my robotic expression dawns on her. "How you holding up?"

Again, I can't help it. I shrug. "I mean, of course I'm sad. But… I also know I did what I could for her, y'know?"

She nods. "I remember you weren't sure about that call, but from what I could tell, you did everything you could."

"So to be honest, that makes me feel a little better. I mean, not *good* because she still killed herself. But if I know I did everything I could do… I couldn't have done anything more, right?"

"Right."

"So, I have to be OK with that."

Maggie nods and gives me a hug, one of her warm moments. I'm fine with it. She retreats and lets me go about logging in to the computer.

It may be cold, but I don't think much about Caroline that shift, nor after. It's not that I don't care. She's the first client I've known, for a fact, has ended her life, and that will always be with me. Usually we have calls that leave us feeling uncomfortable, where we just can't sit right with the resolution, but for once I know the final outcome: This caller has chosen suicide.

But I can't just keep thinking about it. There will always be suicidal people, and there will always be people that I can't help. Some people, no matter how many resources they have, are just going to kill themselves anyway. Working in the crisis business, it's just a natural risk you have to live with. If you can't live with that uncertainty, the not-knowing whether the person will be safe or not, then you need to find a new line of business.

So maybe it's hard or unfeeling. But I re-read my notes for that call with Caroline, and that's it. I listen to others' calls, and I take some of my own. But that's all the time I have to spare on thoughts of that one, deceased caller for today. Right now there are other lives to try and save.

Lacey

Pat, the veteran overnighter, has left the agency to spend more time with what remained of her lungs. That's not a joke: She had "a major health event" and decided to stop working so she could concentrate on getting well. I'd be shocked if she actually gave up the smokes, but hey, I've been wrong before.

Hired to replace her is Lacey. Lacey is a dear but painfully inept at just about everything. She isn't good on the computer, she doesn't know community resources, and she doesn't so much have counseling skills as she does an earnest desire for the caller to be her friend. She means so well that it almost hurts to watch her limp along as she does. Still, she's a warm body in the overnight seat. Well, usually.

Like most people who work overnights, Lacey has a disordered sleep schedule. Normally this would just be her own problem, except that Lacey has a habit of over-sleeping and therefore showing up to work late. At the hotline we have a policy that the bare minimum for any shift is two people, and that's usually how many people are scheduled for the overnight. So when Lacey shows up late, she keeps one of the evening shift people from leaving on time.

I'd heard about this, and now that I was working evenings I was on my guard. But it wasn't until I was dating Grant that her over-sleeping struck me. Of course it was a Saturday night that I was supposed to meet Grant after work. But normally when she was late, you'd give her a call, she'd wake up, and be there in half an hour. Not so that night. I called her every fifteen minutes for a solid hour and she still hadn't shown up. After the first half an hour I had called Meeke to ask her what to do; this made it midnight. Even if I wasn't meeting up with Grant, I just couldn't stay the whole overnight shift.

"Keep calling her," she said. "If she hasn't called or shown up in half an hour… Well, we'll figure it out."

I couldn't call as often as I would have liked because, of course, I had to take calls. In brief moments of quiet I called her. Still, no answer. I flagrantly broke the rules and texted Grant to let him know what was going on. He didn't tarnish the image of perfection I had, and he said he understood and would see me whenever I got out. By and by it came to be one in the morning. I finally had a moment where I could call Meeke again.

She swore. "I thought when you didn't call back that she had come in."

"No, I was on calls. I still can't get a hold of her."

She swore again, a few times. She sighed. "Just hang tight. I'm coming in."

"You're going to take calls?" I gasped. It was almost unheard of, for Meeke to take calls. She might have her part-time job at another hotline, but for us? She was management.

"Dude, it's gotta get done," she said, "We only have so many other overnight people, and they can only work so many days in a row. Give me, like, fifteen minutes. I'll be there."

And so it was. Normally so impeccably dressed, Meeke came in wearing yoga pants, a hoodie, and slippers. She had a large tumbler of coffee clutched in her hand, tight as a claw. Even though I had told Camille what was going on, her eyes still widened at seeing Meeke in her current state.

"Get ready, Camille," Meeke warned. "I'm letting you know now, every repeater is going to get away with getting extra calls, and every protocol is going to get messed up. But I'm hoping it'll be better than nothing."

I made room for Meeke in The Big Girl Chair. As I gathered my belongings, I thought to myself that after pulling this on Meeke, Lacey was so fired.

Except, she wasn't. She was placed on probation, but she wasn't fired. Really the main reason for this was because it's hard to hire overnight people with the specific set of skills needed for this job. She was late multiple times during her probationary period, but it took months before Leann found someone who could fill the void in the schedule Lacey would leave behind.

Lesson: Ineptitude will be tolerated, even when others' lives are on the line, for the sake of convenience.

What She Did

Everyone who works here has a call that sticks with them. It's not even necessarily the "worst" call, the one with the highest degree of danger. Sometimes it's just something that hits you at just the right moment. I was warned that if you have an issue in your life, that's when you start to get calls about that issue. I didn't believe them, brushing it off as superstitious hooey.

The phone rings. I answer. A firm female voice, middle-aged I'd guess.

"Yes, I'm calling looking for information," she says. "My friend recently killed herself, and I'm looking to find an agency like yours where I can volunteer to try to prevent this happening to other people." She's very matter-of-fact.

She sounds sturdy, together. "All right," I say. I gather the usual information we try to get for each call. As I'm pulling the information up, I add, "And I just wanted to say I'm sorry for your loss."

"Thank you," she says brusquely.

"And I think it's great that you're taking your loss and turning it into something to help others."

A small whine is heard on the other end, then a sniffle. Then more. She is crying, and she can't stop.

"I just…" she finally says. "I need to do something! I just think of what she did and I need to do something."

"You are doing something," I reassure her. "That's why you're calling."

"I can't believe she did this… She… She hanged herself in her closet, with a belt. I mean, why do people kill themselves?"

"I wish I had a definite answer for you," I tell her honestly. "There are lots of different reasons, and for those of us left, none of them make sense."

"I just don't understand. I just… I can't help thinking of times we had together, just talking. And I can't believe she never mentioned feeling this way to me. Why didn't she feel she could talk to me?"

"I don't know. But suicide is a hard thing to talk about. She might have found it too hard to bring up."

"And I keep thinking of… Of what she was thinking of before she did it. What she did. Did she put on her favorite outfit? Did she have a cup of tea beforehand, to help calm her down? Did she listen to music?"

I don't know why, but everything she's saying hits me square in the gut. I bury my face in my hands as she talks, trying not to cry. I succeed, but barely. Sam catches my eye and mouths *You OK?* I nod quickly. I manage to keep the tremble I feel in my throat out of my voice.

"I think it's normal to ask all those questions. To wonder about those things, like answering those questions will somehow make it hurt less."

"But it doesn't!" she wails. "It doesn't help at all!"

"I know. How can it? But it's normal, as terrible as it is. It's normal."

I know my words are nothing special in moments like these. Reading them over I know how obvious they are. But in that moment, they help the caller on the other end. She needed to hear that, she says. And she's going to do her best to move on. I give her the number she asked for. The call ends.

It's a queer several minutes, that call. I hear a glimpse at one of my alternate realities, the fate I could have inflicted on my own loved ones all those years ago. It's surreal in a way that unnerves me. I need to take several moments to collect myself after she's hung up.

A Weird Phenomenon

I have never been a morning person, but I need to wake up very early these days. This isn't so much because of my schedule, but because I need time to calm down after I've woken up. You might wonder how a person can need to calm down after they've been asleep however-many hours, but you probably don't have anxiety.

As soon as I woke up, I'd be stressed about going to work, stressed to the point of hyperventilation. About who I was going to have to talk to that day – and then there were the callers. I wish that was a joke, but it was the truth. There were days I'd rather deal with a heavy suicide than my coworkers. The incident with Jenna was likely forgotten by her, but it had left me shaken.

But those calls do wear a person down. I'd been doing this for years now, and that's a long time to deal with a stressful job and a strange schedule. It's hard to pick a toughest call from the week, let alone for over the years. Was it the guy who admitted to molesting his own daughter multiple times? The woman who would self-injure herself vaginally because it reminded her of the times she'd been raped? The survivor of breast cancer who had a reoccurrence of the illness, calling us because she thought we could answer whether or not life insurance would pay out if she killed herself because she knew she couldn't handle going through chemo again? Like watercolors, the terrible tales would bleed together, an awful, muddy portrait of woe.

I'd go to bed weeping, crying because I knew I'd have to face another day with coworkers I didn't like and calls that wrenched my soul. Grant comforted me as best he could, but there was only so much he could do. "So look for another job," he'd say.

But it wasn't that easy: The hotline was very accommodating around my grad school schedule, allowing me to take my classes and start my internship, which right now was with a substance abuse agency and I hated. Pretty soon I'd be able to intern at the rural hospital our hotline was partnered with, which was another opportunity to like what I was doing and possibly change careers. But for now? I felt shackled to that damn phone. For now, at least, I was stuck.

One day I came in for my evening shift and Meeke was still there. I commented it must have been a bad day if she hadn't left yet. She admitted it had been rough. I inquired further.

"I just got off the phone with one of the hotlines I used to work with."

That was odd, but hardly troublesome. "I didn't know you stayed in touch with them," I said.

"Usually I don't, but… Well. We got one of their workers on the phone. As a client. We had to interrupt their suicide attempt."

I was startled. Even though I didn't know any of their people personally, they were fellow crisis workers, and therefore one of my own. "Oh my God."

Meeke nods. "It's actually not all that uncommon among crisis workers. It's a weird phenomenon, but it's not unheard of. We've actually been really lucky here." She shrugs. "I mean, as far as I know. For all I know – well, anyway. I should let you get to work."

Numbly, dumbly, I go to my desk. I sit down and begin to log in, and I realize. I need to get out of here before it literally kills me.

Self-Care

I've quietly been doing my homework. Not for grad school, but for my meeting with Leann. I need the health insurance offered by the company, which is only available to full-time employees. That much I knew, but how many hours is considered full-time? Surely I can cut down from my forty a week a little bit? Yes, according to the company guidelines – that is, the company that owns the hotline: thirty hours a week is the minimum a person needs to work in order to be considered full-time.

This should be a no-brainer to Leann. Marisol has moved to a different position within the hotline, one behind the scenes and thus more appropriate to her absolutely average talents, which has left us short a shift supervisor. I assume Leann would like to keep this one happy by helping her reduce her burnout.

Some of you are surely laughing by now at my childish trust of management's best intentions. You should be, because it really was laughable. When I approach Leann with my proposal to reduce my hours to thirty a week – I even suggest different schedules – she smiles at me tersely and says she knows how important self-care is, but oh gosh, that schedule. It would be so much harder to do it if I had a reduced schedule, and she knows how much I value the company. Confounded, I agree that I value the company and my position within it. She tells me that if I reduced my hours to thirty a week, she'd have to return me to my status as a minion. Her smile gets tighter as she sends me back to The Big Girl Chair.

I hardly know what has happened when I go about my usual business of the day. I had been so sure my proposal was logical. I had been open about the fact that I had been burning out between work and school, but I had expressed a desire to keep doing my best work. I acknowledged that my quality hadn't been up to my usual standards, which is why I proposed this means of fixing it. When Sam and Vena were going through their drama, she was readily accommodated – why were my time constraints from bettering my education treated so unreasonably?

I talked our finances over with Grant, but it didn't take much discussion. We were comfortable, and I had had it. Leann was going to try and call my bluff? Fine.

"I've thought over what you said," I panted, mouth dry from the nerves, about a week later "and I've decided to step down as shift supervisor and go back to being a telecounselor."

Leann's eyes widened, slowly and only a little. If you weren't paying attention you wouldn't have caught it, but I did because I was staring her down. She has just realized that between me and Marisol, she is now short two shift supervisors.

"I need to take care of myself before I can take care of anybody else," I added, nearly directly quoting from the hotline's employee manual under the heading *Self-Care*. "And I can only do that at thirty hours a week."

I smiled tersely.

And so it was: My schedule is reduced to thirty hours a week. I don't find out until the next pay period that Leann decides not to reduce my salary according to my new position because, in a pinch, I can cover for supervisor shifts until they promote new people.

Lesson: Sometimes you really do get to have your cake and eat it too.

Epilogue

If you're like me, you're wondering about the fate of some of these people. I don't know everything – and frankly, not everything is interesting – but I'll share a little.

When Kathi left, she went on to work for an agency for seniors. She's likely retired now. Maggie retired from the hotline to spend more time with her grandchildren. Sam continues to work as a supervisor. She found a much nicer girlfriend and married her. They did not have a rainbow theme, as Sam had thought she would.

Jenna quit the hotline to work selling real estate. She broke hotline rules and accessed every worker's home address, where she mailed her listings. When she left, she gave everyone a business card. I told her I wasn't in the market, so she should save it for someone who could use it. She insisted past the point of reason, and I declined past the point of cordiality.

Sullivan got married to someone who appears to suit him. Mike has had bad relationship luck, but he's still happy and is seeing someone seriously now. I have no idea what happened to the first Grant, nor do I care. Freakin' whippets, man.

And for me? Well, "Grant O yes!" and I got a nice apartment, got married, and got a dog. Meeke spoke at our wedding, and Mike was a part of the wedding party. Meeke is now one of three head honchos at the hotline, where she still works. Leann left the company, though I have no idea where she went.

After the reduction in my hours, I interned at the rural hospital owned by the hotline's parent company. They later hired me, allowing me to finally leave the hotline business… At least, for a while.

But that's another story for another day.

Printed in Great Britain
by Amazon